CHIPD

CHIPD

AMARI RAE PULIDO

NEW DEGREE PRESS

COPYRIGHT © 2022 AMARI RAE PULIDO

All rights reserved.

CHIPD

ISBN   978-1-63730-645-1   *Paperback*
        978-1-63730-728-1   *Kindle Ebook*
        78-1-63730-919-3   *Ebook*

CONTENTS

CHAPTER I

"The only safety concern we foresee at the moment is the capability for external actors to gain access to your private information through these chips."

Mattias Rozelle was on the tenth floor in his cubicle with the other junior engineers working at Chipd. He watched a recently uploaded video of the Commander in Chief's report on the accelerating usage of hand microchips throughout Sweden. The government first suggested every citizen receive a hand microchip last year as technology advances in all aspects of daily life.

"These chips have been disregarded as nothing more than glorified smartwatches. While they are no more than a grain of rice in size, they have the potential to enable a new area of cybercrime if exploited. The Swedish Armed Forces don't yet have the knowledge to brace against such cyber-attacks. Four years since Elias Karlsson founded Chipd and one year since the start of public use of these chips, there have been no known concerns for their physical safety. However, we are taking seriously the potential for external actors to manipulate the chips digitally."

Mattias ended the video and headed to the elevator. He scanned his hand to open the door and once again inside the elevator for admittance to a secured floor, inaccessible to most junior engineers. He had requested and received temporary permission to land on the floor in advance of his first visit a few weeks ago.

"*Labb, nivå två*, lab level two," a monotone voice announced as the elevator door opened on the second-lowest laboratory floor at Chipd.

Mattias entered the lab, calling, "Superintendent!"

"You can call me Nova," she replied matter-of-factly while continuing her work on new hand microchip prototypes. She stood in front of a platform raised to her chest level and wore black specs that jutted out vertically. They stuck to the sides of her forehead with thin bars, and the lens enabled her to view things in a magnified state of multidimensions. Every night in her lab, she wore these specs, designing new microchip prototypes patterned after the original she finalized last year. Thousands of volunteers had opted to receive them since, and now every Swedish citizen is encouraged to use one.

"*Super* Nova," Mattias said, and she smirked at the nickname. "You know, I understand why they keep you down here working on all these minor variations to the hand microchips, but I can't help but sense this repetitive production holds you back."

"From my... true potential?" Nova suggested as she continued her work. Mattias began to respond when she added, "What is it you've meant to run by me, Mister Rozelle? Today is not your first visit." She turned and raised an eyebrow. Her vitiligo gave the gesture an emphasis since her skin color changed just above the brow line. "How may I be of help to you?"

He glowed in the bask of her attention and straightened his posture. "I'm sure you've realized by now the current uses for hand microchips will eventually prove insignificant. A hand microchip can only offer us convenience in performing daily tasks. It can unlock a door, make a purchase, scan blood analytics. A *brain* microchip implantation, however, could—"

Nova rolled her eyes with a grunt and whipped around to resume her work, seemingly more unimpressed than before.

"No, really," he continued quickly. "They would open new doors in artificial intelligence. They could possess features to cure a plethora of physical and mental health issues, elevate the world of digital entertainment, and advance human weaponry unparalleled. If manipulated correctly, they could transfer full sensory experiences, brain-to-brain communication, or character overriding. Brain microchips are the future!"

In silence, Mattias bit his inner lip and shuffled his feet.

"When you got hired to work for Chipd and create these hand microchips, did you think it was absurd then too? Isn't this where it is all leading to, anyway? I am simply suggesting we be proactive in taking the next inevitable step here. We've entered a new era of human augmentation, but brain microchips are where you draw the line?"

Nova placed her specs on the table before her and whirled around. "What are you thinking? I draw the line at mind control, which is not as you say 'inevitable.' And who is this 'we' of which you speak? I would create something the world is unprepared for, and you, a junior engineer, would receive the credit for the idea of my work as I regret what I have enabled them to do."

"Them, who?" Mattias asked softly. He dismissed his question. "This is just my first time mentioning the idea—a draft of an idea. So, I'm going to head back up to my office now." He leaned back and gestured with his thumbs to the elevator door in a slightly playful way. "And, if you'd like to follow up on this sometime, my door for you is always open... *Super* Nova."

Mattias could feel Nova's stare burning through his back as he left the lab. *She'll come around soon enough, and the next time we speak, she'll be coming to me.*

CHAPTER II

ONE YEAR AND TWO MONTHS LATER

MEETING SEBASTIAN

Sebastian approached the door to his apartment, unsure if he was nauseous from soccer practice or because he'd receive the email any day now.

"Do you always come home this late?"

Sebastian was startled by the voice he heard call out to him from the living room. He slowly grinned and sighed a breath of relief before bear-climbing up the stairs. "This is the time I usually come home; I had soccer practice!" Sebastian explained.

"*Well,*" his father spoke, "your coach should consider that you may have other things to do in one day."

Sebastian inspected his father's atypical appearance. His father wore a burgundy button-down with black dress pants, pointed shoes, and a thin silver necklace. His hair was a crown of natural, thick curls that few of the Afro-Latino families in the area grew. And the emerald out-lined glasses he usually used hung from his shirt collar as he read from a website that Sebastian squinted to read.

"Things like what?" Sebastian asked.

"Like…" His father stood and presented himself with arms outstretched, beaming with a sense of pride Sebastian hadn't seen since he kicked the winning goal at a game last year. "Celebrating with your dad on getting his new job!"

They embraced in a long hug and patted each other on the back like Sebastian would his friends after soccer practice. He was proud of his father, who'd spent the past two years struggling to find a better-paying job. It was always a dream of his to get involved with sports-related work.

"I start next week, and on my way home from my inter-view, my third and final interview," his father added in a low voice, "I grabbed each of us one of these!" He held out three aquamarine T-shirts from the Brazil national football team. In the center read "CBF."

Sebastian pulled one over his high school jersey. Wearing two extra-large-sized shirts at once reminded Sebastian to start wearing adequately fitted clothing or gain more arm muscle to fill his sleeves. He could see himself play-ing for a professional team someday if he hadn't already set his sights on studying International Relations in col-lege. "Thanks, Dad."

As his father folded the other two shirts, Sebastian received a notification on his phone. It was an email, and the muscles in Sebastian's face fell as his eyes locked in on the sender.

"Seby?" his father asked, studying him.

Skolan för internationella relationer, the School of International Relations. Sebastian maintained a fixed stare on those words before unlocking his phone to read the email. Sebastian offered no reply to his father as he sat on the couch, his legs positioned like the grasp of an arcade game crane. He was tugging at the green calcite crystal on his necklace from his mother, which lay upon his chest.

Suddenly, his father was standing beside him. "Ha!"

His exclamation sent Sebastian's body into the back of the couch, and he ran his palm over the top of his hair.

"Son, you got it!" He shook Sebastian and planted a kiss on his head.

The email read: *Congratulations, Sebastian Hernandez! We welcome you into Skolan för Internationella Relationer, the School for International Relations in Sweden. We are thrilled to welcome you to our university, which has accepted—* His eyes scanned to the center of the page, already aware of every interesting fact available about the university. *We are also pleased to accept you into our new International Scholar program! The four scholars accepted into this competitive program will commit to studying at the*

He turned to face his father, who was hovering over his shoulder to read along.

"I'm so proud of you. See!" He whacked Sebastian on the side of his head playfully. "And all this time, you were worrying about getting in. We knew you could do it. Just wait until your mother gets home; she won't know what to do with all this news!"

Sebastian stood and let a tear drop fall from his eye when he blinked, past the length of his tall body.

"You can tell her your news first, Seby. Wow!" His father nudged him.

Sebastian smiled sheepishly. "Dad, you can tell her your news first. She knows you had another interview today, and she'll want to know how it went," he counter offered.

"No, no, you can tell her first." His father stifled a laugh as he side-eyed Sebastian, and the two of them continued their competition until the sounds of keys unlocked the front door. They looked between each other and simultaneously bolted to the stairs.

"Babe, welcome home!"

"Mom! Dad has something he wants to tell you!"

Sebastian's mom entered, set her purse down on a step, and rested a hand on her side. She tilted her head back, raspberry lipstick-colored smile and bright copper-colored eyes shining at her husband and son, who were both antsy with anticipation.

"Okay, someone, tell me what's going on."

MEETING LUANNIE

Island Breeze scented incense sticks spread smoke around their cyan-walled room. Seven stories high in a Honolulu apartment complex facing the shoreline, Luannie alphabetized the books of musician autobiographies on their shelves and afterward completed crafting another homemade bracelet. It consisted of beads, stones, and shark teeth that Luannie had collected along the shore just the day before with their younger brother, Koa. They hung it with the growing collection of original bracelets on the wall and began to gather their outdoor belongings for the beach, along with their laptop.

"Let's go!" they shouted in Samoan to Koa as they held open the front door.

A moment later, Koa came running through the door and straight to the elevator in the hallway, clutching a pair of goggles.

"Not so fast!" they shouted after him, but he was already clicking the elevator button.

Not long after they exited the building, Luannie found themself looking out into clear open space with no clutter of industrialization and free of all signs of humanity besides the faint sounds of the city. Tan sand and teal waves moved before them, delivering materials to the shore and taking the coast back out to sea.

Koa was too young to remember the move, but Luannie often thought about their old life in Polynesia, the other third-gender friends they had, and the humble home in which they lived. Their parents moved to Hawaii to be closer to relatives. The two of them worked together for an environmental agency and spent every day leading educational workshops and training teams of volunteers. Despite how unfair it seemed to Luannie to act as a parent, watching Koa race further ahead toward the water, shrinking in size as he blended into the distance reminded Luannie of how much they appreciated their time spent together.

Koa waited until Luannie delivered the hand signal for him to enter the water, a swivel that mimicked a wave. Luannie set up their towels and strolled along the shoreline, bending down to gather shells and feel the texture of the sand. After washing the objects they collected in the water, Luannie headed over to the towels and opened their laptop. A notification from earlier was on their screen but could not open due to the lack of Wi-Fi connection. The message title read: *Application Status for the School of International Relations.*

Suspense took over after fifteen minutes of trying to relax under the sun beside Koa, who was finished swimming. "Koa, we need to head back now." They glanced over at him through their winding waterfall of dark brown hair to see him play with the edge of his towel in one hand and slowly pour sand out from the other. "Koa."

"So soon?" He rolled sand until it clumped between his fingers. "The sand is so soft. What is it made out of?"

Luannie smirked and motioned for help with collecting their things, used to his attempts at stalling. "You want to race?" they asked him.

His face lit up at the offer. "Yeah! You know, I've never run *away* from the ocean before."

"The sooner we return, the sooner I can make you a bracelet," they tempted, hanging onto the last word.

Koa paused for a second before racing toward city land, sending golden dust clouds up behind him.

"Hey!" they chuckled, trying not to trip over the drooping towels.

Koa was fidgeting in the elevator; he loved when Luannie made him jewelry because he could show off the pieces to his friends, who also thought they looked cool. They sent him to shower quickly to give themself time to connect to the home Wi-Fi and check the long-anticipated email.

"I'm going to be super-fast, Luannie! Please wait for me to get out! Okay? Wait for me to get out of the shower before you start!"

The light from the laptop screen lit up their face as their eyes scanned the message that read: *Congratulations, Luannie Manu! We welcome you into Skolan för Internationella Relationer, the School for International Relations in Sweden. We are thrilled to welcome you—* In a split second, a hot wave of emotion rushed over them. They wiped instantaneous tears off the keyboard with their tank top, smiling in gratitude.

"I'm going to take the fastest shower ever! Don't start making it without me, okay? Luannie!"

MEETING JAEWON
Jaewon overheard his mother arguing with his father down the hallway from inside the bathroom, finally telling him to leave. His father had been seeing another woman for several months now. Jaewon had found the other woman's purse in his father's office and brought it to his mom last month, but she told him not to worry about it.

Now, his mother stood in the hallway, looking up at her husband with indifferent eyes. "You don't have to say anything. Now, leave with what you need. You've already hurt us enough," she spoke firmly in Korean.

He refuted, "You have never understood my life. I have responsibilities outside of this home! How can you ask me to leave when I am the reason we keep this place?"

His mother asked his father again to leave, discouraging him from any acts of resistance. Slowly and quietly, he obeyed and began to pack his essentials into suitcases. She clarified that he had chosen to abandon his family by emotionally, physically, and financially investing in another woman.

Jaewon finished drying off in the shower as he heard his father preparing to leave the house, unsure whether to stay in the bathroom until he exited.

His father called out to him, "Good luck getting anywhere now! If you need help, ask your mother!"

Jaewon held the towel to his cheek and scrunched his face, allowing the pain from the past few months to escape. He only began to relax with the realization that not only was the secrecy gone, but his mother had rightfully redeemed her dignity. He knew he could not stay in the bathroom until the coast was clear because there was no way to assume how much longer his father would take. Reluctantly, he pulled on his pajamas and exited the bathroom, cautiously maneuvering into the kitchen where his mother had already prepared food.

"Please, eat. I'm sorry I didn't warn you; I honestly didn't expect to do this today."

Jaewon kissed his mother and silently took a seat at the dining room table, trying to remain composed as she followed him to push back his bangs.

"I love you," she said.

Jaewon smiled because he loved her too and began to eat his bibimbap.

Anxiety has always served as a trigger for seizures due to Jaewon's epilepsy. Watching his father peer into the kitchen as he finished his bibimbap without saying a word reminded him of this. His head lightly jerked backward as his breath and hands began to tremble, and he feared having an episode. Jaewon listened as his father descended the stairs.

Thump! He heard the sound of glass breaking.

From the floor, Jaewon saw his father rush into the kitchen. He felt the bits of glass that pierced parts of his skin, fidgeting in a semi-conscious state. His father ran over frantically but paused just as quickly. He stood tall, took a deep breath, and returned to the stairs.

Jaewon kept his eyelids parted to watch his mother rush into the kitchen. She pivoted toward the stairs with tension but returned her attention to Jaewon and squatted down to help him. "You're okay! It'll be all right. I am here, Jaewon," she rambled. "I'm right here."

It took a minute to get Jaewon situated upright and leaning against the kitchen wall. He sipped on a glass of water and picked the remaining bits of glass from his forearm. Although Jaewon felt like releasing his emotions with tears, he began to laugh. He wasn't sure why. Then he pressed his lips together, lifted off the floor with his mom's help, and got back onto the chair.

안녕, he thought, staring at the table. *Bye.*

His phone alerted him of a new email, and when he saw the title, he knew he needed to open it right away. Jaewon and his mother moved outside to the balcony that extended from their kitchen. He pulled back a chair for her to take a seat and swooped down to embrace her into a hug. "You deserve the best," he whispered.

"I already have it," she said, pinching his chin as he retreated.

Jaewon sat across the table and exchanged a knowing glance with his mom. He saw hope in her eyes where he thought there would be hurt. Her eyes glowed not from the moon's reflection but a place of inner light. And her whole face radiated from the smile her lips formed. Jaewon couldn't help but smile back as he pulled out his phone to read the School of International Relations message.

"나는 에 있어," he said. "I got in."

She further widened her uncontrollable smile, which he returned. They sat on the balcony, digesting the events that had, in an instant, enormously changed both their lives.

"These are good things happening," she assured him. "Looks like you have that good luck your father wished you earlier."

Jaewon glanced at her, slightly surprised at her sense of humor but even more so at her detachment. He giggled as she sent him a wink from across the table.

MEETING SAMARA

Samara was making history, beating her father in a competitive game of Turkish Draughts for the first time. Circular black and white pieces filled the board, and Samara slid one of her white pieces to the left. Her father, grinning at her move in response, hesitantly made a move with one of his black pieces.

"You've improved!" he exclaimed with pride in Arabic.

Samara spent at least half an hour each weekday with her father before he continued his work from a private at-home office. Samara would spend more time with her mother, but she was always traveling on business trips, so seeing her mother return home felt like receiving visits from a distant relative. Nonetheless, Samara's parents cared deeply for each other and their daughter, despite her tendency to be unconventionally outspoken.

Her parents shaped Samara well in adolescence, and, in turn, she also influenced them greatly during her upbringing. Her parents were Muslim, along with approximately three-quarters of all citizens of Qatar. Sharing the Islamic faith was a significant way their family and many others connected throughout the day, praying together and sending meaningful Quran passages over text. She truly enjoyed the lessons she learned from scripture and kept an open heart to Muhammad's teachings. Her parents struggled with Samara's passion for questioning her faith for the sake of seeking the truth without fear of finding new answers, something she strived to do in everything.

Sitting across the living room coffee table, she grinned as her father said a prayer for victory under his breath, but she did so even wider when she made the final game-ending move.

He flipped the board jokingly and threw his hands in the air as she laughed at his over-the-top demonstration. "That's okay; I prayed you would win," he said.

A phone ring interrupted and pulled her father away to take the important call.

Samara adjourned to her room, the walls covered in original artwork she created in her spare time. The centerpiece image depicted nature in a personified manner: the breath of wind, the veins of water, the skin of dirt, the eyes of fire, and plenty of space for the respected intangible. Her phone alerted her of a new message. She sat upright at her desk chair and prepared to resume a new drawing of Qatar's skyscrapers when her curiosity made her glance at the message notification banner on her phone. She rushed into the living room, where her father was intently listening to the person on the other side of his business-related call.

Samara bounced on the balls of her feet, paced to her room, and back into the living room again. Her father raised his eyelids and poked his head forward, requesting some form of nonverbal communication from her to indicate whether or not there was an urgent matter that held precedence over his call. She calmed down a bit and stuck her phone into her pocket.

Then he whooshed past her, down the hall, and entered his office for privacy where he was never to be bothered.

Samara pursed her lips and responded to her mother's message that stated she would be home tonight in time for dinner. Her mother had gone on a business trip to Europe that had kept her away for over a week. Samara wanted to let her father know, but she was happy at the thought of him being pleasantly surprised. Immediately, she headed into the kitchen to start creating her mother's favorite dish, which took just under an hour to cook: thareed. Their traditional thareed recipe contained fried vegetables in a vegetable broth-based stew with spices and bread.

Quickly, Samara wiped her hands on a towel, used the same towel to wipe the stove and counters, and set three plates at the dining room table. As she sprinkled garnish on the finished dish while swaying to soft folk music pouring out of the radio, she heard the front door slam shut.

"Samara, look at you!" Her mother grinned and sniffed the mouth-watering aroma that had permeated throughout the house. She tenderly tucked a strand of Samara's hair back into her Shayla, something Samara typically wore in the presence of non-mahrams. Samara wore her Shayla in front of immediate family members when expecting visitors or preparing to perform salat. She put it on while making dinner because once her mother forgot to mention that she had a guest with her, a lesson that had stuck with Samara ever since.

Samara's father entered the kitchen and cheered at the sight of his wife. "We have a lot of catching up to do! Nine days is a long time. Too long!"

"Yes," her mother responded. "Exciting new project, and I am blessed to have the opportunity to be involved with this." She looked at Samara as she removed her Shayla. "And you, too, Samara, will have exciting new opportunities starting in life, I am sure."

Samara checked her phone at the dining room table and read the introduction to a new email from the School of International Relations before her father intentionally cleared his throat. She calmly placed the device on the window ledge beside her without saying a word. As they ate in their usual food-revering silence, Samara paused from her meal, looked between her parents, and lifted another forkful of delicious thareed to a subtle smile.

CHAPTER III

The celebratory welcome email sent out to the four International Scholars contained a link to a video chat invitation through *Connected*, a conversation app for overseas communications. After answering unorthodox security questions such as "What is your top bucket list activity?" and "What is your strangest hobby?" all four students were able to confirm their accounts. Sebastian, Luannie, Jaewon, and Samara stared at the Connected main menu page, hesitant to join the meeting room in their respective homes across the globe.

It had been two weeks since Sebastian received his acceptance email into the program, and he didn't know what to expect from the other cohort members. He entered the room and noticed only two others shared their video while Samara supplemented turning on her camera with an image of herself.

After a moment of silence, Samara turned on her audio. "مرحبًا! Hello!" Sebastian followed suit by saying hello in Portuguese, then Luannie in Samoan, and Jaewon in Korean. Samara continued, "I think it's just us here today so we can get to know each other. Although, it would've been nice to see one of our directors too. Is everyone planning on sticking with this program?"

Sebastian watched Luannie pull their thick hair into a messy bun as they said, "I'm so excited to be in Sweden for the next year with you all. I couldn't let this opportunity pass me by."

"Yes, I can't wait to get to know each other! I've always wanted to travel and study International Relations, so this is a perfect match for me," said Jaewon.

Sebastian peered around his screen at the other students, noticing their environments. He saw the homemade bracelets hanging on Luannie's wall, the vegetables behind Jaewon in his kitchen, the city behind Samara in her picture. Then he became aware of his background—a large dresser with photos of him in different soccer uniforms over the years.

Sebastian chimed in, "Do we want to go around and do some introductions? I can start. I'm Sebastian, he-him-his, and I'm from Brazil. I love playing soccer," he said, leaning to the side to show the photos behind him.

"Glad to meet you! My name is Samara, she-her-hers, and I am from Qatar. Hmm..." She looked upward and searched her thoughts. "I like drawing and cooking for my family."

"That's cool! My name's Luannie, they-them-theirs, and I'm from the Polynesian island of Niue, but now I live in

Hawaii. I also like drawing, and I spend most of my free time outside, reading, or making jewelry."

Sebastian noticed a similarity between Luannie and somebody he had been friends with since elementary school. It may have been their low voice or the calm, cool, and collected personality he picked up on.

"I'm Jaewon, he-him-his, and I'm from South Korea. How cool it is that we are all from different places! It's nice to meet you all. I like to play video games, but I can't think of anything else to share right now."

Separately, in a private chat, Sebastian received an individual message from Samara. He furrowed his eyebrows as he skimmed the message skeptically and then proceeded to close the chat window, forgetting that his video was on as he rolled his eyes. *That's the first thing you ask someone you've just met? Mind your business.*

The message read, *Isn't it great that this program is so affordable? Paying only thirty thousand in BRL a year is excellent for a bachelor's degree, including two semesters to study abroad. If you're interested in applying for any scholarships, I'd be happy to help you find some!*

Sebastian created a private chat of his own and sent a message to Luannie. *It's wild how much you look like a friend of mine.*

Jaewon moved straight black strands of hair away from his forehead. "So, did you all apply because of the location or the major?"

Sebastian replied, "It was both for me. I knew I wanted to study International Relations, but I wasn't sure if I'd be able to go abroad. My high school counselor advocated this program to me, so I gave it a shot, and here I am." He was in good spirits, but he recognized the nervous tone of his voice did not convey this, so he flashed a smile.

Luannie laughed. "Agreed! I knew what I wanted to study but had no idea this opportunity existed. I also learned about this program through my high school. I wonder how many people applied since there are only four of us?" they asked.

Sebastian received another notification from a private chat. Disappointed, he read, *Anyway, being away from family might be hard. Are you close with yours? I think living on your own is the best way to shape yourself as an individual, in my opinion.* He looked again at the picture of Samara on-screen before closing her chat window a second time.

"Yes," Samara confirmed, "just the four of us. For some reason, we must have stood out to them in a pool of applicants! We are a pretty diverse group."

Sebastian received a notification from Luannie in a private chat. *Really? Awesome. If you want, let's talk again sometime before we get to school!* He smirked as he read the message and wondered if the others had noticed.

There was an awkward silence in the meeting room as the scholars searched for discussion points to make. Sebastian spoke up to break the tension, "Since this is a meet and greet, and we've already done greetings, let's get to the meeting part. Maybe we can each send an anonymous message in the chat with a fact about ourselves and then guess who it's about."

Samara turned on her video and adjusted the camera then her Shayla. She sat in a solid white room with no decoration on the walls. "That sounds good," Samara agreed and muted herself as she typed.

Two messages appeared into the general chat box, and then a third. After a few seconds more, someone sent the fourth message, and Jaewon took the role of reading them aloud. The first one said, "My friend and I have matching palm tree tattoos on our ankles." Jaewon looked around his screen. "Should we guess now? I'll say Luannie."

Samara seconded Jaewon's guess, but Luannie shook their head. "Nope! I don't have any tattoos. Oh! Koa!" they complained as he popped into their room.

The scholars giggled at the commotion as Sebastian raised his bent leg into the air and held it until the camera focused on the outer side of his left ankle. "There it is. I don't live near the coast, but I love it." It was a black outline of a palm tree with light detail work in the trunk and leaves. "And hello to your friend there," he joked to Luannie.

"That's my brother, Koa. He's a little—" They were interrupted by infectious laughter. Koa approached the screen and waved at the scholars.

"Hi, Koa!" Sebastian yelled.

Luannie spoke to Koa softly in Samoan, and he left the room after waving one more time.

"How cute!" Jaewon said and, without skipping a beat, eagerly read aloud the second message in the chat. "I accidentally ended up in a movie because I walked past the actors during filming." His mouth turned into the shape of an "O" as he waited for the others to share their guesses first this time.

"We have an actor in our midst," Samara joked. "Luannie, is this you?"

Luannie shook their head and pointed at the screen. "Jaewon, I think I recognize you from somewhere. Did I see *you* in the background of a movie scene?"

Jaewon smiled sheepishly and raised his hands. "You got me. It was a small film, and the road was left unblocked during filming, so they caught me in the background and kept that take!"

"That's pretty cool," Sebastian remarked, bringing the side of his face close up to the camera. "Can I get an autograph?" He saw that Jaewon was shy from the attention, so he added, "Well, you'll have to show us sometime when we're together. There's only two left now," Sebastian referenced the remaining messages.

Jaewon read the third message to the group. "I have never seen snow, but I hope to someday. Oh." He frowned. "Which of you two have never seen snow? Samara?"

Four pairs of eyes darted around the screen, waiting for a response from somebody.

"I'll say Luannie then," Sebastian threw in a guess.

There was another beat of silence before Luannie said, "I've never seen snow either, Samara."

Samara unmuted herself and pinched her shoulders up to her neck. "I love the heat, but I've only ever seen photos of the snow. I want to feel it, and I want to see how everything looks covered in it, and I want to play in it too."

The scholars smiled, and Sebastian realized that the remaining message must belong to Luannie. "Sweet, and I'm sure someday you will. That also means that somebody here wants—"

Jaewon cut Sebastian off in excitement to say the last message, "I want to become a traveling explorer and make discoveries across the world!"

The other three scholars looked at Luannie on screen with widened eyes.

"Wow," Samara said, "that's quite a goal. Why do you want to do that?"

Luannie picked at their nails and twisted a few outlying pieces of hair. "I don't want to travel like a tourist; I want to live like an adventurer. People visit places never knowing their history, and I want to find more pieces of history in different places."

Sebastian nodded in approval of the idea and leaned back in his seat. He was exhausted from a long day of playing soccer and cleaning, and it was past three in the morning in Brazil. His eyes burned as he strained to keep them open. Nonetheless, he tried to remain attentive to the conversation. "So, what time is it for the rest of you?" he asked.

"It's only eight at night for me," Luannie answered.

"About three in the afternoon in South Korea," Jaewon said.

"Eight in the morning—oh, hold on…" Samara paused. "Nine in the morning here. My mistake," she corrected herself.

The students spent another twenty minutes discussing courses, destinations near the School of International Relations, and how they all related to not learning much Swedish yet.

Before hanging up, Luannie exchanged phone numbers with Sebastian along with the message, *Text me sometime. Maybe after you get some sleep.*

These people are pretty cool, Sebastian thought as he saved Luannie as a new contact on his phone. *Only five more months until August!*

CHAPTER IV

AUGUST

Luannie descended the escalator from the luggage pickup area and searched for Nathaniel in the lobby, awaiting the sight of their housing unit and life outside the airport. They spotted a tall, sharp-jawed man with *The School of International Relations* written on his shirt along with the university's logo. The logo was a globe of the world made out of electrical currents.

He approached them with a tote bag, lanyard, and class pamphlet. "Välkommen, Luannie! How lovely to meet you. I believe you are going to love it here. Sweden is a beautiful country, and the School of International Relations is a wonderful university. How was your flight? Did you get here all right?"

They couldn't stop smiling—his eyes were a shocking shade of lime green. "Yes, thanks. That was a long flight, but it went by fast. I've been so excited to get here," they said choppily.

His eyes glimmered. "We're so glad to have you here. As I wait to welcome Jaewon once his flight arrives in a few hours, please, allow me to show you around the area, and then I will take you to the place you will call home for the next year." Nathaniel flashed his eyes open. "Oh! Since you are the first to arrive, you get dibs on choosing your living space."

Luannie put their new T-shirt and pamphlet into their tote bag, laced their arms through the straps, and said, "I'm ready!"

Meanwhile, Sebastian was unpacking the car with the help of his parents at the Guarulhos International Airport in Sao Paulo, Brazil.

"Baby, I'm so proud of you. If I keep thinking about how proud I am, I may start crying again," his mother squeaked.

"I'm not gone yet," he said.

She stretched out an arm to place her hand on the handle of a rolling suitcase and brought her other hand to her face as she blinked rapidly to hold back tears.

"You're going to do amazing things, Seby. You'll see; you can do anything…" his father choked. Then he pretended to adjust an invisible collar on his shirt and shifted his tone. "Just keep your schoolwork first before you start traveling over there, Sebastian."

Before heading to the airport entrance doors, Sebastian brought his mother and father into a hug, which they seemed delightfully startled by. As he walked away, he turned around to see his father holding his palm up in the air, and his mother shouted, "Love you, *mijo!*"

A few hours later, in Sweden, Jaewon arrived at the airport. He was heading to the luggage conveyor belt when he noticed an older man struggling to lift his suitcase as it was moving along. Nobody around offered to help as the man grasped onto his luggage, which dragged him a few feet. His cane tilted until its base lifted off the floor. Jaewon slid across the floor to catch the older man as he fell, and a few people were staring now.

"You okay?" he asked.

The man turned to look at Jaewon and slowly distorted his face. Jaewon stood to offer a hand, but the man whipped his head in the opposite direction. Then the older man got on all fours and struggled beneath his cane to lift his weight. Jaewon still had his hand extended when the man swatted it away in anger. Forcefully, he uttered a slur Jaewon had not heard spoken aloud before, an insult that wasn't intended for South Koreans but was spat at him now, nonetheless.

A flashback to high school came to his mind when he opened a letter from his international pen pal. Jaewon was speaking with a boy from the United States. As the end of the semester came to a close, so did their correspondence. The last letter Jaewon sent included a photo of himself to his pen pal, John. They were finally exchanging pictures with each other after speaking for several months. The conflicting response made him feel ill, and he never showed it to his teacher or either of his parents out of embarrassment.

Jay, it's been cool talking to you these past few months. I told all my friends about you, and they can't believe all this time I've been friends with one of your kind. You write English so well I honestly had no idea you were Chinese. I kind of wish you'd told me sooner, though. My teacher says my pen pal assignment is over now, so I wish you the best. Good luck with whatever plans you have in your country after graduation.

Sincerely, John.

Typically, their letters were a couple of pages long. John had never mentioned he was white, only that he was American, and Jaewon never felt the need to disclose his nationality or whereabouts because John never asked. After that, Jaewon would only allow people to refer to him as Jaewon, not any nicknames like Jay.

Standing in the airport with thirty sets of eyes burning into his cheek, shame flushed over him as his hand stung from the whack of the man's cane. Nevertheless, Jaewon assisted by grabbing the man's luggage and placing it by his side.

The man grumbled into his watch, and shortly after, a small hologram showing vital statistics appeared in the air on his wrist. The pixels weren't as sharp as Chipd promised, but it was the first such watch Jaewon had seen that displayed a hologram. Jaewon walked past the man as he checked his blood pressure and body temperature on the wristwatch, peering toward Jaewon before he left his view.

Jaewon took long strides to the lobby, wanting to exit the airport quicker than his legs would allow. His tempo slowed as he made his way through the revolving doors that brought him to the sidewalk just outside the main terminal. Cars, taxis, buses, and bikes rode past him. His body became frigid, and he feared he would have an episode. His mind went blank, and he softly swayed in place as a figure sharpened into his view.

"Jaewon?" Nathaniel asked.

"Ah, yes, sir." He spoke wearily and extended a hand out to Nathaniel, who grasped it and gave a firm shake.

"Are you feeling all right? Come on; I'll show you around town a bit and take you to your new home. One of the other scholars has already arrived." Nathaniel handed Jaewon his university-themed gifts and guided him to the parking garage with concerned eyes.

Back in the housing unit, there was a knock on Luannie's door. They felt tired after the jet lag and spending time with Nathaniel, although they couldn't recall where he took them. Their mind was foggy, and they wanted nothing more than to fall into a deep sleep, but the knock repeated itself. Reluctantly, Luannie opened the door.

"Samara?"

"Hi, Luannie," Samara responded. "It's so nice to meet you in person." She took a glance around the room. "How long since you've gotten here?"

Luannie rubbed their eyes and let out a wide yawn. "Oh, an hour or two, maybe? I'm not sure; I'm so tired. How about you?"

Samara let herself in. "I've been waiting for someone else to arrive! I've never left Qatar; I can't believe I'm here right now. I've never been this far from my family or for this long."

Luannie nodded in agreement. "Yeah, I'm going to send photos home later after I catch up on some sleep. Is your room nearby?"

Samara hadn't stopped smiling since the door opened. "Yes! I'm not too far." She took a moment to look around the room again before offering to help Luannie unpack, to which they politely declined.

"Okay. No worries! I'll see you later," Samara responded, exiting Luannie's room.

Somewhere over the ocean, Sebastian watched a Swedish movie on the back of the seat in front of him. He chose Portuguese subtitles to follow along, but it was difficult to concentrate on the storyline with a baby's cries nearby. There was always a crying baby on a flight. The screams pierced through his headphones, and he couldn't turn them up any louder, so he peered out the window and played with his necklace.

His mother had given it to him because she paired crystals with affirmations. However, he was discouraged by his father growing up from manifesting, or "casting spells on rocks," something Sebastian never understood. He used to accompany his father to church services every Sunday, and Sebastian watched a priest cast blessings on the water to make it holy, wine to make it blood, and bread to make it flesh. Not only this, but his father then filed into line to consume the flesh and blood of a sacrificial lamb. Sebastian wasn't sure why his father accepted certain practices of witchcraft and not manifestations, but it didn't stop him from exploring them further with his mother. It was almost like a secret the two of them shared. Sebastian clutched onto his necklace, similarly to how his father would take his rosary, and allowed himself to rest as the cries of somebody's unhappy child traveled through the plane.

A few hours later, Nathaniel took a seat in the airport's lobby for the last time today. Sebastian was late. An hour late. And Nathaniel did not know how to contact him. After all, if Sebastian did not connect to the airport Wi-Fi, he would not see the email Nathaniel sent to him. Nathaniel decided it would be best to remain where he said he would be if Sebastian were looking for him.

Near the food court in an aisle of tourist shops, Sebastian stood, enthralled by a book he picked up in a small souvenir store. He was already three-quarters through when an employee asked if he would be making a purchase anytime soon. The employee called him "buddy."

Sebastian looked between the employee and the book. "Uhm. I'm just about done."

The employee stood tall, teal eyes vibrant against her mustard yellow hair. Freckles lay on her cheeks and nose. "Sir, I'm going to have to ask you to make a purchase or leave. You're in a store, not a library."

Sebastian looked back to his book and scoffed, trying to stop himself from sharing any of the brilliant comebacks in his mind. He shut it with his hand, placed it back on the shelf, and headed out into the rest of the airport. At this point, he lost all sense of direction and could not recall what signs to search for to get to Nathaniel's designated meeting spot.

Shortly after, Sebastian saw somebody rise from their seat out of the corner of his eye. He looked at the man awkwardly, analyzing his sharp facial features. "That must be him," he said to himself and walked toward Nathaniel.

They met one another halfway, and then both took in long breaths.

"You must be Sebastian. You're the last of the scholars to arrive!"

"Yes, that's me." Sebastian couldn't help it, and he let down his guard with a smile.

"Well, then, these are for you. Gifts from the School of International Relations!"

Sebastian's smile grew as he took his gifts. Something about the excitement of being in Sweden mixed with receiving gifts from Nathaniel made him want to laugh. "Thanks." He chuckled. "These are cool. I'm thrilled to be here." *Thrilled to be here?* He looked away for a moment.

Nathaniel patted him on the shoulder, ultimately ignoring Sebastian's late arrival, and began walking out to the revolving doors. "Now, I'm afraid you don't have much say in which room is yours. But they're all the same, anyway. Would you like to sniff out the area before heading to bed?"

"That'd be nice, thank you," Sebastian said.

Back in the housing unit, there was a knock on Jaewon's door, but he was too tired to answer after taking his third and last anti-epileptic dose of Phenytoin for the day, so tired that he missed the second or third knock. He especially did not hear the door as it softly opened.

CHAPTER V

The following day, Sebastian woke up to his last alarm in a rush to get ready. A slight pressure on top of his head, along with the fatigue from last night's sleep, carried over to morning as he stumbled across the room. He watched his bobblehead reflection in the faucet as he thoroughly brushed his teeth with the water off until needing to rinse. Sebastian still couldn't comprehend missing his first two alarms. It was four minutes to 10:30 a.m. when he ran into Luannie in the hall.

"Luannie," he said, pleased to see them a few steps in front of him.

"I'm surprised we're not late," they replied. "I was worried I'd sleep through my alarms. The last one got me up."

As they walked in front of him, Sebastian noticed their height difference. If he was six foot three inches, then they must have been five foot seven inches. He remembered how peers bullied him for his comparatively exceptional height growing up but quickly let the thought pass his mind.

A young woman was outside the apartment building with Samara and Jaewon. Jaewon watched as Samara intensely showed the woman how to locate her hand microchip. Samara was feeling around the skin when she accidentally hit the woman's watch, and a small hologram appeared over her arm, showing the time was 10:29 a.m. Jaewon excitedly began telling the story of an older man at the airport who used a similar device.

"Last but not late," Sebastian assured Luannie.

"Welcome, scholars. It's nice to meet you all finally! My name is Aria Mariani, and I am one of your program directors. I believe you all met Nathaniel Olsson yesterday at the airport, and later this evening, you will be meeting your other program director, Millie Olsson," Aria shared in a thick accent.

Italian, thought Sebastian.

"I see some of you are already using your School of International Relations tote bags," she remarked, smirking at Sebastian, who was the only one without his. He gave a playfully guilty smile. "Soon, we'll be taking a bus to… Stockholm!"

The scholars showed immediate interest. Sebastian had wondered whether he would get to visit the Swedish capital during his studies. He remembered researching the Vasa Museum, the Skansen, the Drottningholm Palace, and Gamla Stan. But the words his father left him with at the airport rang through his ears, reminding Sebastian that classes would become his main priority as soon as they began.

"On the way, please fill out the online questionnaire I will be sending you. The notification will appear on the School of IR app that comes with your new phone plans. It won't take long; we need to be aware of any allergies, medications, or medical conditions you may have. Now, I understand the itinerary we sent over the summer was rather vague. Millie, Nathaniel, and I have worked together to create a wonderful set of excursions for you to participate in over the next week!"

Aria shuffled around in her pocketless tote bag, making Sebastian glad to have brought a book bag with plenty of pockets.

"Here. I have with me pre-programmed, university-sponsored SIM cards for your phones. Please note that the card will disable your phone's previous number and service plan. You can all insert these now and feel free to ask me any questions or talk amongst yourselves until the bus arrives," Aria pressed a button on her watch and read the hologram that rose into the air above it, "in five minutes. It looks like it's going to be a beautiful day today!"

The scholars inserted the SIM cards into their phones, half the size of a traditional SIM card. Sebastian fumbled with it between his fingers and questioned why nobody inserted the chips on their behalf.

"Oh, and when you remove your chips from their packaging, give them a moment to scan a piece of your fingerprint," Aria mentioned, answering Sebastian's unspoken question.

Within milliseconds, their phones automatically downloaded contact information from one another, and names with headshots shuffled rapidly on their screens. The SIM cards automatically downloaded software, including an app titled Chipd with the image of a microchip, an app titled School of IR with the university's logo, an app titled Uppsala Map with a location pointer on a grid, and an untitled image of a crown in the middle of a sword pointing upward.

Sebastian was chatting about the picturesque scenery of Gamla Stan with Luannie when Jaewon approached them. He looked as if he were about to address Luannie when he became distracted and glanced at the road. During the pause, the others looked over too and saw the bus had arrived.

"Hey, Jaewon," Sebastian said.

Jaewon cringed. *Is Jay all right with you?* he imagined being asked.

"Am I saying your name right?"

Jaewon smiled and nodded.

Everyone boarded the bus, and Sebastian ultimately decided to sit with Jaewon since he hadn't gotten the chance to speak with him yet, not since their virtual meeting over the summer. Luannie took a seat in front of them, accompanied by Samara.

As Sebastian listened to Jaewon share his passion for an upcoming video game release, he overheard Samara circumvent small talk with Luannie and directly begin asking questions about their personal life.

"Was it difficult for you to move to Hawaii from your island in Polynesia? That must've been challenging for you," Samara asked. Jaewon mentioned something about skiing when Sebastian listened to a follow-up question from Samara. "I mean, permanently moving to the United States and now traveling to Sweden, you must feel so detached from your roots. Would you consider returning to Polynesia someday?"

Luannie's mouth hung slightly open before starting their online questionnaire. All they said to Samara was, "I'm sure both of us will enjoy our time here."

Sebastian nearly bit through his tongue as he gave an "mm-hmm" to Jaewon, redirecting his attention toward him for the rest of the ride.

It took about an hour to get from Uppsala, the fourth-largest city in Sweden, to Stockholm, the largest city in Sweden and most populous in Scandinavia. The bus stopped on a busy street that was four lanes wide. A crowd waited at the crosswalk until the sign turned green and the road filled with a blur of moving colors as people crossed past one another.

"Everyone up? We're here!" Aria exclaimed. "I apologize for my silence during the ride. I've been looking over your questionnaires and finalizing this afternoon's plans. Let's get going; somebody is waiting for us outside."

All four scholars shared the same curiosity as they hurried off the bus.

Nathaniel clasped his hands together like cymbals, and Sebastian couldn't help but giggle; the exaggerated expressions in Nathaniel's face while speaking were amusing.

"Hello, scholars, nice to see you again. I'm glad you've made it here to the capital safely. Today, I will be guiding you on a day trip to Stockholm! Now, it's…" Nathaniel pressed his watch, and a hologram popped up with the time, location, and weather, "11:45 a.m. We're going to eat and have a traditional Fika experience, then visit the Vasa Museum, and from there view the art in the subway on our fifteen-minute ride to Gamla Stan where we will end our day in front of the Royal Palace."

"Luannie," Sebastian whispered.

They turned around and began walking with Sebastian behind the others on the sidewalk.

"There's a light coming from your phone," he said, nodding toward their tote bag.

They dug out their phone and read the message from Jaewon, which said, *Would you like to eat together for Fika?*

Luannie looked up at Jaewon, who looked back for a response, and they mouthed the word "yes."

A few minutes later, the six of them reached a bustling café. Confectionery smells leaked from the pores of the restaurant's windows, luring anyone within a mile toward its doors. Although the heat from summer was likely to last into winter with the expected temperatures higher than they'd been a decade before, the aroma of brewing coffee made Sebastian feel even warmer.

Sebastian watched as Luannie accompanied Jaewon, Samara took a seat with Nathaniel, and he took a seat by Aria.

"Sebastian! Thanks for joining me," Aria said.

"Hi." He glanced around the café at the people making conversation, inspired to start one. "Did you attend the School of International Relations too?"

"Oh, I am not an alumnus. Nathaniel is an old friend, and he told me about this position while I was job-hunting. I'm glad to be working here, especially since I get to work with the inaugural cohort of International Scholars," she explained giddily.

"I read in the acceptance letter that we'll all be in the same classes together." Sebastian's head nodded to the two tables where the other three scholars were seated. "I'm interested in all the courses, but will we have a chance to meet any other students?"

"Well, the School of IR is an online school, so this program is specifically designed for the four of you to have hands-on experience with our faculty and staff while having the opportunity to immerse yourselves into Swedish culture. But I'm sure once you complete your year of in-person studies, you'll get to meet other students in the rest of your online classes."

Sebastian picked up a menu from the table.

"I know this cohort is small," Aria continued, "but the ratio of students to professors will greatly benefit all of you, and you all seem like a great group of students."

He flipped a page, nodding slightly.

"Give it time," Aria said, leaning forward. "This is your first official day here. Classes don't start until next week, and you'll have plenty of time to get to know the other scholars."

A waiter left Jaewon and Luannie laughing together about pronouncing the items on their menu before heading toward Aria and Sebastian.

Aria continued, "I understand how difficult this can be. You are away from friends and family with many strangers in a new country, and it's overwhelming. So, if you need anything at all, I am here for you."

Sebastian smiled and looked up from his menu. "Thank you," he said sincerely. Then he ordered a coffee in the best Swedish he could pronounce.

Lunch was a social experience, talking in between the chewing of swirled pastries drizzled in colored icing, washed down with coffee that featured latte art. Sebastian's drink had a leaf design, and Aria's had a cat. Half an hour passed by in five minutes when Nathaniel waltzed by Sebastian, waving his arms in a "come hither" fashion.

"Does that mean it's time to go?" Sebastian joked to Aria.

The Vasa Museum was no more than fifteen minutes by bus. It stood near the water on Djurgarden island, and a slight breeze carried over to Sebastian's forehead when he got off the bus, cooling beads of sweat the air conditioning had not been able to keep from dripping. It was the hottest year in recorded history, as was the year before that. Sebastian noticed he was not the only person wiping perspiration onto his clothes as the six of them approached the building.

Cool, he thought, quickening his step.

Nathaniel assumed his tour guide position and spread his arm through the air across the length of the warship inside the museum. "The day Vasa left Stockholm was a Sunday. Most passengers boarded the ship a few hours after church service, most likely praying for a safe journey. Strong winds tilted the ship, and water entered through its gunports, which is why it sank within only minutes after setting sail. Some swam 120 miles back to shore, some got picked up by a small craft, but most of the thirty who died were trapped inside—including one of its two captains..."

Sebastian knew all this because he remembered the research he had done over the summer. His eyes drifted toward the three-meter-long lion figurehead at the front of the ship. The buzz of Nathaniel's educational spiel continued in the background.

"They later discovered the major flaw in the Vasa's design was due to it being top-heavy. However, had the gunports been closed, the ship most likely would not have sunk. Nobody received punishment for sinking the Vasa to prevent embarrassing the king who had approved the ship's design. Everyone involved eventually got promoted! Here stands the Vasa today," he used both arms this time to cover the size of the ship, "finally discovered in the summer of 1956 by Anders Franzen, about 330 years after the disaster."

Sebastian noticed where Nathaniel knew to pause for effect when speaking, something at which politicians or theater kids were excellent. He wanted to spend more time than the forty-five minutes they spent at the Vasa Museum, but it was already 1:20 p.m., and they still needed to see the old town, Gamla Stan. They were all heading to the nearest subway when Samara struck up a conversation.

"Sebastian, we're still strangers."

He matched her gaze, unsure of how to respond.

"Are you usually this quiet? I'm not usually this talkative. But I don't want to miss out on the full experience of this opportunity. You know?"

"No pressure; we'll all get to know each other over the year." He smiled because he realized he had echoed Aria's message to him earlier.

"Well, it's nice to see you with a smile on your face. I haven't gotten the chance to speak with you much. I met Luannie last night, but I think it was pretty late when you and Jaewon got in, and I was the first one here."

Sebastian thought about Samara's interrogation of Luannie on the bus ride to Stockholm and instigated one of his own. "So, are you missing home yet? You were born and raised in Qatar, and it must be hard being away from your family and friends for the first time." His eyebrows dipped down along with his mouth into a pout.

"Yes, thank you. I'm sure I can get through the ups and downs, though," she responded swiftly.

"Same here, same here," he confirmed.

Samara went to adjust her pants but awkwardly brought her hands together to crack her knuckles instead. "So, what was high school like?"

Sebastian snorted at her persistence to make conversation, and the noise surprised him. He began giggling. He'd never snorted before, but something about being asked what high school had been like while he was halfway across the world to participate in a unique college program was like asking an athlete at the beginning of a tournament how their years of training had been.

"Wasn't too bad."

"Oh, no?" She was still looking up at him, bright-eyed.

"Why do you want to know? To see what clique I belonged to?" Sebastian asked confidently.

"No," Samara said with a slow blink. "I don't care about any of that."

He thought about his high school experience before deciding to elaborate a little further. "It was fine—I mean, it was juvenile. I didn't go to the best of schools, and the best of people didn't go there either. But I graduated in the top twenty of my class, top three on our soccer team, and haven't looked back since getting on the flight here. I might miss my friends a little." Sebastian looked over at her, still looking at him. He wiped his face with the top of his shirt and proceeded to walk in calm silence to the subway.

They reached the subway entrance, and Nathaniel stopped everyone by a bench. "Okay! How are we doing?" He exchanged eye contact with everyone individually. "All righty then," he said with a snap and the accent of a young Jim Carrey. "Let's jump right into it. The tunnelbana, Sweden's subway system, features the most extended art gallery in the entire world! Here is one of one hundred stations featuring art from the mid-twentieth century. It will only be a ten-minute ride to old town Gamla Stan where we will take a walking tour, and you can purchase vintage souvenirs. Keep in mind, Gamla Stan is one of the best-preserved medieval city centers in all of Europe, so do please enjoy your time!"

The escalator delivered the scholars underground, where the interior of the subway tunnel emerged into view. A simulation of teal water and its aquatic life encompassed the subway station's walls. The fish switched into X-ray vision, so the contents of their stomachs were visible— human waste. They reverted to their original appearances, and Sebastian watched as a load of plastic permeated the water surrounding him. A few of the fish chased after the plastic; a few got stuck in the debris. Then, a large oil spill turned the color of the water black, and the fish rose to the top. There was a sound of movement along the floor as the simulation reset itself to the beginning, which began before Sebastian descended the escalator.

The beginning repeated and featured an iceberg, which jutted out into the subway, rumbling the floor. It drifted away into smaller pieces that moved along the walls, two with single polar bears who were noticeably malnourished. Then, the icebergs disappeared back into the walls as the ice melted, raising the water levels to engulf the entire ceiling.

We create simulations to raise awareness about this, but not solutions to stop this? Sebastian thought.

CHAPTER VI

Jaewon felt both puny and giant after watching the ocean simulation, which he could still see through the subway doors. He noticed Samara step up beside him as the subway began to move and was eager to share his thoughts with her.

"That simulation is wonderful because you don't just see it. Walking through, I smelled the saltwater, heard fish swim, felt cool air—it was all so real. A simulation that lives and makes people sense the art they're in."

Jaewon knew he was more intrigued by the subject than Samara, so he paused, but she nodded with an expression that encouraged him to continue.

"Imagine how an advanced version of that simulation can be useful for international relations. It could help people understand what other people are going through." He looked off for a moment. "It could let somebody feel like they're taking a vacation without traveling! Incredible. But it would only be as real as you allow it to be. If you keep reminding yourself that it isn't real, then you wouldn't be able to appreciate it." Jaewon smiled at the floor. "I want to create an art simulation that gives people the full-body experience of what it is like to ski in Pyeongchang county. I've wanted to go since 2018 when the Olympics were there. It isn't far from Seoul, I think maybe two hours, so I will be going there with my mom when I return to South Korea!"

Samara nodded politely for the rest of the ride as Jaewon explained how simulations could be more realistic than virtual reality.

When they arrived at the station nearest to Gamla Stan, Jaewon smelled wet dirt in the air. A simulation portrayed activities beneath Earth's surface with worms and other creatures Jaewon couldn't identify wiggling in the ground. The soil appeared dry, unhealthy. He poked at the wall that had a squishy texture and mechanical movement to imitate life. Then, he pulled out a water thermos from his School of International Relations tote bag as he watched acidic rain permeate through the mud of the simulation, killing the insects and ending the mechanical movement.

Everyone approached an escalator shaped in a spiral to prevent crime and reduce overcrowding on the upper streets. Only one person could step on at once, and the steps made three 360-degree turns on the way up.

"These escalator models were structured this way to prevent accidents, and they allow anyone who doesn't yet have a hand microchip to find where they are on a map," Nathaniel explained, tapping on the plexiglass that enclosed the escalator. An interactive map of Stockholm with a "You Are Here" pointer appeared, along with nearby locations. "You can also use the Uppsala Map app on your phones."

"As some of you may already know, thousands of Swedes began volunteering to use hand microchips last year. Now, nearly everyone uses them in the country, and other nations are considering the technology. Each chip is unique to its user. For example, my heart rate, blood pressure, body temperature, current location, bank account balances, emails, text messages, home, car and work keys, and more are all stored on mine! It enables me to go places hands-free, and it provides higher security from computer hackers. I also have my wife's information here in case there is ever an emergency. The chips are available to foreigners too. The Swedish Armed Forces and Public Health Agency document all personal information. You will have the opportunity to receive these microchips as well, but we will talk about this later."

Wild, thought Jaewon, feeling at the flesh on the top of his hand.

Jaewon stepped onto the escalator and admired its rotating design. About mid-way through the ride, he saw a man appear two steps in front of him. The man was close, facing down at Jaewon. He watched as the man adjusted the wrists of the sleeves on his suit. The man's blank expression shook Jaewon to his core. He inhaled and contemplated how he could escape the escalator, peering through the transparent plexiglass below him.

Jaewon banged on the plexiglass desperately, turning the map of Stockholm on and off. He let out a scream that pierced the escalator and faintly traveled through the subway below. Then he could hear his name from beneath him as he squatted in place, trying to steady himself on the steps as they revolved around a turn.

The man scrunched his face in anger, bangs similar to Jaewon's hanging in front of his forehead, as he raised Jaewon by the shoulders. Then he shook him and lifted a palm into the air.

"Stop it, please!" Jaewon squealed in Korean.

Jaewon wrapped his arms around himself as the escalator reached three-quarters of its route, the light from outside shining down. His father swooped his palm around, smacking Jaewon and sending him back.

Leaning against a plexiglass map of Sweden with a hand on his cheek, Jaewon grabbed onto the neck of his shirt, wept into its collar, and pleaded, "Leave me alone." The view of his father before him grew smaller within a black outline as he felt himself fall slowly out of consciousness.

Jaewon opened his eyes and saw Aria bending over him. He could feel his legs hanging off a bench, the pain from the hits he took on the escalator stinging in his face.

"Hey, can you see me? Are you feeling all right?" she asked.

Jaewon looked around at everyone, and they all looked back at him incredulously.

Jaewon whispered, "I can't believe he came here."

"Who came here, Jaewon?" Aria asked.

"The man who hit me." He winced in pain as he sat up. "How did he know I was here?"

Aria looked to Nathaniel, and he rushed over to Jaewon. "Did somebody hit you while we were in the subway?"

Jaewon looked at him in disbelief. "You were there!"

Nathaniel jumped back, and Jaewon looked over at the scholars. "Samara, didn't you see him? My father attacked me on the escalator."

She looked between Jaewon and Nathaniel and then shrugged to Aria.

"Okay, why don't you sit here for a moment and drink some water?" Aria suggested. "Where are you hurting?"

Nathaniel cleared his throat and motioned for Aria to come over, and she dismissed herself temporarily.

"It says here he has epilepsy," Jaewon heard Nathaniel say in a low tone, pointing to his phone.

"Yes, it says on his questionnaire that he takes medicine for it. Do you think he should have some of it now? If he even has it with him…" Jaewon struggled to hear Aria respond.

The discussion grew faint until they unanimously peered over at Jaewon, who quickly looked at the other scholars. He hadn't realized his peers were surrounding him with parted lips and staring eyes.

"Should we find medical care?" Jaewon could hear Aria ask.

"Nobody saw a man near him on the escalator. Besides, the steps are so narrow. How could somebody—his *father* have walked down backward to hurt him? Either he's starting to see things, or he's making this up for attention."

Jaewon bit his lip when he realized that if he could hear Nathaniel, the other scholars could too.

"He's probably missing his family," Nathaniel added.

They returned to where the scholars stood around Jaewon and asked him if he had any medicine that he could take. "For seizures," Nathaniel whispered in an attempt to keep the personal information confidential.

"You think—" Jaewon paused. "My father just attacked me in public. I think I know what my father looks like."

Sebastian shot Luannie a concerned glance.

"I'm sorry, Jaewon, but there was nobody in front of you. I would've seen them," Samara said.

They were all silent for a moment as Jaewon stood and grabbed his tote bag. He looked around and noticed they were in the town of Gamla Stan.

"Jaewon, isn't there a chance that maybe you had a seizure and dreamt that your father was with you on that escalator?" Nathaniel proposed.

Jaewon glanced at Luannie as he made his way over to Aria and quickly put his head down. "I need to call my mom before we start the tour."

Aria offered to speak to her for him, but he said that she only spoke Korean. Nathaniel offered his phone for Jaewon to use since the scholars had not yet received phone numbers with their new SIM cards.

As Jaewon explained to his mom the situation in Korean, he noticed the others watching him intently. Jaewon shifted himself, ran his hands through his hair, let his head tilt back, and closed his eyes. After insisting he did not have a seizure for the final time, the call ended, and he promptly took his medicine as his mother advised. He silently removed medication from his bag and chased it down with a gulp of water from his thermos.

Nathaniel put his phone back into his pocket and spoke about the historic "town between the bridges" when Jaewon returned to the group. Jaewon didn't make eye contact with the sets of eyes that lay upon him; instead, he kept his eyes stuck on Nathaniel until they started to burn, and they watered when he finally blinked.

A tall woman with pale blue eyes and whitish-blond hair pulled into a neat top knot approached the group. Despite her elegant aura, she had a strut that could stomp footsteps into the concrete. The woman lifted a hand to greet Nathaniel, then Aria, and smiled at the scholars before singling out Jaewon to pull away.

CHAPTER VII

After the trip exploring Stockholm, Sebastian, Luannie, and Samara were sitting together in the multi-purpose room of their housing unit, across from Jaewon's room. They looked at a series of photos they had taken in front of the Royal Palace on Samara's phone. There was a feature that displayed the photos mid-air in three-dimension before them.

"Does anyone else think Nathaniel jumped out of a cartoon?" Sebastian asked, thinking back on the day's excursion.

"He's a character." Luannie smirked. "I like him."

"I think that was the most entertaining tour of Gamla Stan I could've imagined taking," Sebastian said as Samara scrolled through a few other pictures. Luannie laughed at one where Nathaniel asked them all to make a silly face. The last photo was taken by Nathaniel so that it could include Aria, and she posed with the students as if they were in a line of bridesmaids. She blended in so well that it was difficult to tell whether or not she was a student herself.

"How was it?" Jaewon chimed in, joining the other three scholars on the couch. He appeared as healthy as before the incident on the escalator, albeit a bit rejuvenated after rest.

"Jaewon!" Sebastian reached his hand over Luannie to pat him on the back.

"Where have you been? You missed Gamla Stan, and neither Aria nor Nathaniel would tell us where you went," Luannie frowned.

"Well, our other program director, Millie, was supposed to meet up with us for the tour, but she wanted to take a look at me after my supposed 'episode.' We came back here, and she's been looking out for me in the medical room since," Jaewon explained.

"The medical room?" Sebastian asked.

"Yeah, it's at the end of the hall. I think this whole hall is ours. Our keys only give us access to the fourth floor of the building. Millie pretty much told me she thinks I had an episode due to my epilepsy, but I don't think so."

"Oh, you have epilepsy?" asked Samara.

"Sometimes I blackout, but what happened on that escalator was *real*. I mean, I *felt* it happening to me, and I could still feel the pain after I woke up on the bench." His eyes wandered as he drifted out of thought.

"Whoa. Well, I hope you're able to figure things out."

"Thanks, Samara. I wish I could've walked through Gamla Stan and visited the Royal Palace with you all. I would've been fine enough, but it's all right. We still have a year to explore and take pictures together!"

"That's right, buddy," Sebastian affirmed as he reached over Luannie to pat Jaewon on the back a second time, prompting Luannie to shoot him a glance of warning.

Jaewon stood and peered out of the window above where the other scholars sat on the couch. "Millie thinks I miss my father, and I told her that wouldn't explain what happened to me. Plus, I don't miss my father."

There was silence. *I miss* my *father,* Sebastian thought.

"Are you afraid of him?"

Jaewon looked over at Samara solemnly, and Sebastian looked at her irritably.

"I'm not as scared of what he can do to me as I am to know that he cares so little about what happens to me. Or my mother," Jaewon shared.

Luannie couldn't find words, so they stood to join Jaewon in a brief hug and suggested they all go to check out the medical room.

"It's locked because they keep medical supplies in there and a weird set of chairs. It's basically a doctor's office. Nothing too interesting, but..." he started comedically, "I did get a couple of stress balls from Millie if anyone wants to give them a try."

The scholars filled Jaewon in on the tour of Gamla Stan and the regal atmosphere of the Royal Palace as they walked into the hallway. Then they all dispersed and headed back to their rooms, Sebastian squeezing onto one of the stress balls he got from Jaewon.

It was already seven o'clock at night when Jaewon held onto his stomach and released a small burp in bed before taking one of his pills. He got up to open the refrigerator and saw a few health bars, compliments from the School of International Relations. Their odd flavors varied from cotton candy stardust to oatmeal orange burst. "Just an episode," he scoffed under his breath. "I know my father when I see him."

In their room down the hall, Luannie heard a knock at the door.

"Hey! What's up, Jaewon?" They inhaled a whiff of his strong cologne, a scent they couldn't quite place but smelled refreshing, nonetheless.

"Hey." He crinkled the wrapper of the oatmeal orange burst bar in his hand and brushed back his bangs with the other. "I know you all probably got something to eat already, but I was wondering if you could—or if you'd want to—go find some food?" His voice quickened and heightened as he finished talking, barely getting the words out, and he laughed at himself.

Luannie stepped backward to grab their tote bag. "Let's," they responded with a smile.

He peered around at the walls of their room and admired the dangling homemade necklaces and bracelets. An accessory box filled with supplies of seashells, beads, and strings sat on the desk. A few items sat out as though a new piece was soon to be in the making.

"Oh, those are my jewelry pieces. I've made jewelry for people for as long as I can remember. When I was younger, my father always brought me to the shore so we could go collecting things, and I guess that's always stuck with me. Now I do the same with my little brother, Koa!"

Jaewon smiled as he panned his view around the room, continuing to admire their colorful and creative work in detail.

Luannie walked over to a necklace with a blue stone and shell pattern and took it off its hook on the wall. "Here, this is for you, Jaewon. Just, please," they paused, "be careful with it."

Jaewon thanked them and took a moment to slip the necklace over his head delicately. He looked at it from different angles in the mirror before complimenting Luannie on the handiwork. As they both exited the building searching for food, Jaewon kept looking down at the necklace hanging around his neck.

It was warm outside as they walked past humble houses to the nearest restaurant. The sides of the buildings hugged each other in Uppsala, with striking green leaves sticking out over the roofs from the trees behind. The Fyris River wasn't far away, and its coolness carried over to the neighboring streets through the breeze. The sun was still setting down from the day, which it wouldn't do entirely at night in the summer in Sweden. The sky faded from blue to pink, with swirls of white clouds spotted throughout the sky. It looked as if a painter added them to a completed canvas as a last-minute thought.

"It's not too cold," Jaewon remarked about the weather after a moment of walking in silence.

Luannie rolled their eyes. "Tell me about life back in South Korea."

"Well, I'm not sure what to share. Living in the capital is great and all. Seoul is amazing because it's lively, modern, and old, and there's always something to do. But I also wonder how my life would be different elsewhere."

"Elsewhere..." Luannie trailed off. "I also want to live life elsewhere—in fact, everywhere. I wonder how life differs for people across the globe. Do you have someplace in mind you might want to go?"

"Anyplace. My favorite parts of where I live are the temples and markets. Cities aren't my favorite settings, but I bet people who live elsewhere say the same about where they're from."

"I relate to that," Luannie added. "I grew up in Niue, a small island in western Polynesia, and it's pretty close to Fiji. Life was modest, and I felt more in touch with my family and friends there, even more in touch with myself. But my parents wanted to move to Hawaii for work, and now we live in the state capital. I love Honolulu too, although it's no surprise my favorite part is the beach nearby. I adore the water."

They walked the rest of the way without saying much until they reached Herman's Restaurant, which featured daily items outside their sample menu board.

"Do you want to try this place?" Jaewon suggested.

"Yes!" Luannie's enthusiasm surprised Jaewon.

The busy restaurant had a front wall made entirely of tall windows that were all slightly propped open so customers could dine in a partially indoor, partially outdoor experience.

They took their seats and looked over the menus when Jaewon noticed Luannie staring outside. "Well, look at that," they said.

He turned and saw Nathaniel and Millie entering the restaurant.

Nathaniel made eye contact with them and smiled as broadly as someone could without parting their lips. "Hello, you two!" he exclaimed, a bit surprised.

Jaewon quickly whispered, "Luannie, I think it may be awkward if we all sat together."

"I see you're already checking out the area! This place is great; we come here often," Nathaniel gestured to Millie.

"Don't mind us." Millie extended a hand with long white nails. "Nice to meet you, Luannie. Sorry I wasn't able to be with you in Stockholm earlier. I'll be seeing all of you tomorrow for our second group excursion!"

Luannie awkwardly smiled as they retreated their hand from Millie's embrace. "I'm looking forward to it."

"Jaewon," Millie redirected her attention, "I hope you're feeling better."

"Great," he replied. "I'm also looking forward to finding out the plans for tomorrow."

"Well, you two enjoy your food. We hope you have a good night, and we'll be seeing you in the morning!" Nathaniel shouted as he waltzed away, sweeping Millie along with his arm.

Jaewon and Luannie shot them both with slanted smiles.

Luannie darted their eyes and muttered, "Her hand is freezing." They pressed their fingertips together and looked at the menu uncomfortably.

"I'm not sure," Jaewon said without looking up.

"Huh?"

"—if I should get the meatballs and potatoes or this open vegetable sandwich." He pointed to a photo. Then he quickly answered for himself, "Oh, definitely..." Jaewon cleared his throat and attempted his best Swedish accent while butchering the pronunciation, "Köttbullar med potatismos."

Taken back, Luannie burst out laughing and quickly covered their mouth, only to laugh again.

Jaewon blushed, remembering how they had also found it amusing when he tried pronouncing menu items at the café in Stockholm earlier. "I'll keep practicing my Swedish," he said, hiding his face behind the menu.

CHAPTER VIII

Samara stared at her outfit reflected in a tall mirror as she wrapped her hair the following day. A video message was sent to the scholars through the School of IR app on their phones. It showed a hologram of Nathaniel's pixelated face as he exclaimed, "Five minutes! I'll see you all downstairs!" Samara chuckled at the sound of his chipper morning voice. *How is he always so upbeat?* Samara loosened a piece of hair from her Shayla to lay with a wave over her forehead and took the elevator down to meet the others.

"Hello, hello! Good morning, everyone." Nathaniel's eyes shined as he clasped his hands together. The whites of his eyes were as bright as his teeth.

"Thank you all for waking so early. As you can see, it's a beautiful day outside. We will be visiting your school's 'campus' this morning for a brief orientation! Since most of our teaching is typically online, our 'campus' is a humble collection of small offices and classrooms." He motioned quotation marks with his fingers each time he used the word "campus." "You will officially be meeting Millie, my wife and Aria's fellow program director. You may have seen Millie when she arrived in Stockholm to accompany Jaewon back to the housing building. Afterward, we will be seeing the Uppsala Cathedral!" Animated, per usual, he looked around at everyone's blank faces. "Hmm. Okay, who is tired here?"

All of them mumbled, and Sebastian said, "Bad dream. I tossed and turned for a few hours."

Jaewon raised his hand in agreement.

"Ah, so we didn't get enough sleep. I know a few of us went out exploring last night," Nathaniel gazed imploringly at Luannie and Jaewon, drawing looks from both Samara and Sebastian. "A brisk morning walk to 'campus' should help us with that!"

Sebastian lowered his head and stifled a smile at Nathaniel's repeated use of air quotations.

"Let's get going! And don't worry, there will be lunch when we arrive." Nathaniel smiled as a look of excitement spread across their faces, all except for Sebastian's.

"I wish I was that positive first thing in the morning. I wouldn't be surprised if Nathaniel's already had three cups of coffee," Samara joked beside Sebastian.

"Uppsala Cathedral," he muttered back as they started walking. The housing building sat perpendicular to the block that led straight down to the campus building.

"Yes, it should be nice." She held eye contact with him, but it remained unreturned. "My family is Muslim," she shared, intruding on his thoughts. "I've seen the wonderful ways our faith can connect people, but I know religion can be used to separate people as well. I personally think it's healthy to accept not to know someone who already knows everything and the possibility that there isn't something to know."

Sebastian was silent. *I don't think I should get into this.*

"You don't seem very excited. Are you disappointed because you wanted to go to a different place?" Samara asked.

He cleared his throat as they continued following Nathaniel down the narrow, store-lined street toward their "campus." "I don't follow any organized religion. It's not that I didn't try hard enough in the past; I just don't believe in any, and there are no compelling reasons for me to," he said calmly.

He looked up and over at the trees that lined the sidewalk as he drew in a long breath, tapping his index finger to his thumb.

Samara searched for what he may have seen in the trees. Still watching the view behind him, she said, "That's perfectly okay."

"I don't want to live life for an afterlife or the ghost of anyone else, either," he added. A noise left his mouth as though he would add something more, but instead, he stared straightforwardly.

Samara tucked in her lips, tilting her head. "Do you think any world religion has it right? Or do you think that no one has known the ultimate truth?"

"If there is one, it likely isn't as human-centric as most universal religions were designed," Sebastian replied. "I think a lot of religions are metaphorical stories that people created to understand the science of the world." He rolled his head around, stopping halfway to stretch his back. "And most people never thoroughly question their faith because there are no valid answers; that's why they need faith in the first place." He looked off again and let the left corner of his mouth sink into his cheek, where a small dimple formed. "But those are my thoughts. I think it's harmful to worship anything."

Samara was unusually silent as they walked past a garden store, the smell of lavender permeating through the air. The breeze that carried the smell also sent a hair over her eye, and she gracefully swiped it back.

To combat the silence, Sebastian filled it. "My mom spends time with crystals every day, and some people find it silly to put worth into them. I asked my father about it once, and he said it was witchcraft. I didn't say it then, but I wanted to tell him that he believed in witchcraft too. I watched him and other members of his organization form circles and cast prayers hand in hand. They recited spells to summon spirits in their midst. But when I questioned his faith, he told me to pray for my answers." Sebastian chuckled.

Jaewon and Luannie turned around to see why he was chuckling, with Luannie searching Sebastian's face to detect his mood since he seemed to be in a rather engaging conversation with Samara at the moment.

"Love is stronger than any of my parents' differences. That's why they work together," Sebastian said.

Jaewon and Luannie turned back around in unison and continued their conversation.

Samara slowed her speech. "Sebastian, in the greater scheme of things, I do believe society is changing for the better. People are more and more willing to challenge belief systems by accepting new facts, or a lack thereof." She moved strands of hair to the side of her forehead again as the wind picked up. "Would you mind telling me about what you *do* believe?"

Sebastian smiled; it was the first time he could recall Samara asking someone if she could ask a personal question, something he'd hoped she would work on improving.

"I appreciate the nature we are." He rhythmically tapped on his necklace and held it out for her to see. "I don't need a book to give me a reason to exist along with everything else in the world." With a kiss, he tucked his necklace into his shirt.

Sebastian watched as Samara intentionally stepped over every crease in the sidewalk, and he irresistibly began doing the same. Even *trying* to listen in on Luannie and Jaewon's conversation couldn't distract him from his overworked subconscious now.

"Do you have a headache? My head has hurt since we got here, but I don't want to take any medicine for it," Samara told Sebastian.

"Hm? Oh." He finished counting the cracks he stepped over on an even number. "Yes, me too. But I think it's easing up." He thought back on how he'd ignored Samara's private chats to him during their virtual group meeting a few months ago and felt terrible about perhaps judging her forthrightness too soon. "Thanks for talking with me about this—" he began to say.

Suddenly, Jaewon seemed to have tripped over a potted plant that sat outside a storefront. He barely got the chance to extend his arms in front of him by the time he had hit the ground on his left side. Nathaniel whipped around, and Sebastian joined Luannie in rushing beside Jaewon.

"Hey, are you all right?" Sebastian asked, his eyes fixated on Jaewon, but he didn't answer right away.

"Oh, dear, let me see what's happened here." Nathaniel lifted Jaewon's head and could feel a wet warmth. A little blood. Quickly, he positioned Jaewon upright to lean against himself and took out a thermos of water. "Samara,

Jaewon hit his head when he fell. Would you please message Millie on the School of IR app and let her know we're going to be a bit late? She's waiting for us to arrive."

Samara nodded as Luannie's hands covered their mouth in shock at the sight of blood on Nathaniel's hand.

"He'll probably be okay. It wasn't too far of a fall," Sebastian tried to assure Luannie and himself.

Nathaniel had to motion for several concerned bystanders offering assistance to move along, although he did accept a few napkins to press against Jaewon's head and then clean his hands.

"Drink up." Nathaniel gave Jaewon some of his water, and the cold shocked him, jolting him forward.

"Easy, Jaewon. You're all right. It looks as though you've tripped and hit your head on the sidewalk. Are you okay?"

Jaewon peered up at Nathaniel, the other scholars, then at the few strangers around him. "I'd like to get up now, please." His face was devoid of emotion and focused on nothingness as Nathaniel reluctantly helped him up.

"Are you sure you don't want to rest for a moment?" Nathaniel suggested.

"I'm okay to keep walking," Jaewon responded. When nobody did anything but stare at him, Jaewon began walking again, and Luannie speed-walked so quickly to keep up that Nathaniel had to race in front of them both.

Sebastian rose from where he had been kneeling and took a steady breath before accompanying Samara, who finished sending Millie a message about what happened. His eyebrows furrowed inward as he ran his hand over his head. He pulled out his cell phone from his pocket and sent Jaewon a message, to which he received a short response of *Fine, thanks.*

They stopped in front of a two-story building lined with bushes. Tan and brown brick were layered smoothly with a new front door and window sills that made the building stand out from the others on the street.

Nathaniel ran both hands down his silk jacket to smooth it out. "Scholars, this is where your classes will take place over the next year of your studies! As you can see, we have renovated the building to make sure it is equipped to best suit your academic needs. Millie will be taking you on tour through the building, and she also has lunch waiting for you inside. Please, let yourselves in, and Millie will be out to see you all shortly."

Nathaniel unlocked the door with a swipe of his hand and held it open for them. He didn't follow them in, but they could hear the latch of the door locking as it closed behind them.

"This should be fun." Samara tried to break the awkward silence.

Sebastian looked around the campus lobby. The school name and logo were on the wall to the left in Swedish, with multiple translations listed underneath. On the opposite wall was a large television. They all stood patiently, waiting for Millie to come in and join them. The silence was awkward as Jaewon stood with his hand holding the side of his head, looking down at the floor. There was an interview on television where a Chipd employee named Mattias Rozzelle shared an idea about evolving the current usage of hand microchips.

"Aren't those the same kind of microchips that Nathaniel and Aria have?" Luannie asked.

"And most Swedes nowadays," Sebastian noted.

"I'd never put one of those things under my skin. An electric key instead of one that needs physical turning is one thing, but sticking it inside of your body?" they said.

"Would you ever get a tattoo or piercing?" Samara asked.

"Maybe. My body may not need those either, but tattoos and piercings don't carry the same risks as a microchip. Tattoos and piercings add something to the body to make it look different. Hand microchips are inserted into people's bodies so they can live physically and intellectually lazily," Luannie explained.

"And more conveniently," Samara suggested as she ran her hand over the television, turning it off, "as all technology does, I suppose."

Luannie looked between Samara and the television.

"Hey," Sebastian started, taking a step closer to the TV.

"The microchips can do many things, such as turning certain appliances on and off if programmed to." Samara waved her hand over the screen again, and the interview with Mattias Rozzelle resumed. He was discussing the possibility of a microchip that gets inserted into the brain.

"It's cool that people have learned how to create such technology, but I'd rather just press a remote button to watch television." Luannie peered down at Samara's hand. "When did you get that?"

The squeak of a door opening grabbed the scholars' attention by the wall opposite the television, and Millie stood beside the school logo.

"Hello," she greeted the scholars. "I hope I haven't kept you waiting long. Let me see if I have this right." Millie pointed to each of the students as she said their names and pronouns aloud. Each of them nodded afterward, except for Sebastian, who was still wondering how she had appeared so swiftly.

"All right," she proceeded with an air of collected confidence. "Nathaniel informed me that Jaewon got hurt again. Before we move further, how are you doing, Jaewon?"

Jaewon licked his lips and avoided eye contact without saying a word. Luannie's eyes laid upon him.

"Let me know if you'd like to take a break at any point. It's no problem." Millie sized up each of the scholars after Jaewon didn't offer a response. "Well, isn't this an interesting bunch! I know it's only been a couple of days, but you'll warm up to everything soon enough. Now, if you'll follow me, I have a lot to show you here." She smiled for a few seconds before turning around and walking through the open door frame from which she had appeared.

Sebastian realized the knobless door had moved up into the wall above the door frame.

When none of the scholars moved to follow Millie, Samara turned to Luannie and said, "After you."

As Luannie turned the corner into the connected room from the lobby, they looked back to make eye contact with Sebastian and made a face that said, "Whoa."

CHAPTER IX

The scholars entered a room lined with tables and four armchairs at the center. Virtual reality goggles, whirring monitors, and other gadgets made by Chipd filled the tabletops, while each chair had unhooked straps on the armrests. The smell in the room was the combination of a new car, cleaning supplies, and Millie's intense perfume, somewhat off-putting but intriguing, nonetheless.

"These are like the chairs I saw in the medical room," Jaewon remarked so softly, Luannie could barely hear.

"Before you begin classes, you will need to be able to access the campus doors, lockers, and vending machines on your own. As you may know, foreigners can receive the hand microchip now. The School of International Relations has received approval from the Swedish Migration Agency to administer them to our students! In your welcome letter over the summer, we mentioned that microchips are in use nationwide and that we would explore your ability to have them. Since you all have student visas and will be residing within Sweden for a year, you are legally considered temporary Swedish residents. That qualifies you for the chips," stated Millie.

Millie noticed Luannie's face flush and said, "They are free, painless, and are removed before your return home. If anyone is unable to be chipped, there are alternative solutions. However, we strongly advise receiving a chip, seeing as most things nowadays are becoming more accessible by chip than manually." Millie led the scholars over to the chairs and placed her hands on one of the headrests. "Here with us today, we have an exceptional guest from Chipd. Her name is Nova, and she will be placing your chips today."

The scholars waited in silence, expecting Nova to enter the room.

Millie laughed and assured them, "Soon. She will be here shortly. In the meantime, I would like for you all to go over and sign these digital release forms that enable Chipd to place your chips and connect your personal information to them. The chips also send daily updates to the Public Health Agency of Sweden to monitor the population's statistics and to detect any urgent issues in an individual. "

Jaewon walked over to Millie, expressionless, and extended a hand to take one of the tablets with an open release form.

"Great!" Millie sighed. "Who's next?"

"I've already received mine, actually," Samara murmured. "It was one of the first things I wanted to try when I came to Sweden."

"That's all right, Samara. We can link up to your information with the Public Health Agency later today, but I'll still need you to sign one of these release forms for the School of International Relations." Millie wiggled a tablet as an invitation for Samara to grab hers. "Sebastian? Luannie?" Millie observed as the two of them peered around the room, eyeing the technology.

"I feel overwhelmed," Luannie admitted. "Can I sit for a moment?"

"Certainly. I'll let you read these release forms while you relax. If you are nervous about anything, please feel free to ask me." Millie turned to Sebastian, who was looking at a screen on the wall. An image of the silver and white-toned twelve-story Chipd Headquarters building sat on-screen with a forward arrow waiting to play a video.

"That for us?" Sebastian asked.

"I'm glad you asked." Millie turned outward to address the room. "If you'll all take a seat, I have a brief presentation to show you now. This video explains what a microchip can do, how many people are using it, and how the placer will insert it." She waited for the scholars to seat themselves and resumed the video while standing behind the chairs.

Luannie sat next to Jaewon. "What's up with you?" they whispered to him as the presentation started.

He turned his head down to the left toward Luannie, shaking it slightly.

"Are you homesick? You know, if you need something, you can tell me." Luannie looked back at the presentation, which showed the quick insertion of a hand microchip. They winced in disgust. "I'm worried about you," they added. Luannie felt the pressure of Millie's eyes fall upon the back of their head, and they redirected their attention to the screen.

After a moment, Jaewon shared, "I didn't trip over that pot earlier."

Luannie looked before them. "Did you have another—"

"Another episode?" he interrupted, asking them. "I saw my father leaning against that storefront, right in front of me... It was a surprise, but my feet didn't fumble over anything."

"Ahem." Millie cleared her throat, and while it sounded as though it came naturally, it reminded Luannie that she was still standing behind them.

"Are you going to mention it to Millie? She might be able to help you," they proposed.

But Jaewon scoffed. "She'll dismiss it as a symptom of my epilepsy again. Something weird is going on, and it doesn't make any sense."

He was quiet for a while, as was Luannie, who massaged the top of their head to relieve a persisting clump of pressure. *Jetlag,* they thought. Luannie kept Jaewon in the corner of their eye but couldn't bring themself to say anything more.

Loud music blared from the screen as Millie scrambled to turn the volume down a few notches. The man referred to in the video as a "placer" was making direct eye contact with Luannie through the screen. The placer's gloves then grabbed a small brown hand and rubbed disinfectant over it. He pushed back a bracelet on the boy's wrist and successfully inserted a hand microchip with a long silver tool. *That bracelet looks like something I've made before,* they thought.

"Thank you," Luannie heard a familiar young voice tell the man in Samoan. Then they saw the boy, curls framing his face, and he was staring at his hand in awe. Koa passed the camera as he moved out of line for the next person to take their turn.

Luannie's mouth opened, and their esophagus went hot as they jumped out of their seat, but the presentation had quickly moved onto the next segment. Their chair flew back a foot or so behind them.

"Luannie? Do you need something?" Millie asked as everyone looked between them and the chair, which now lay
on its back.

Luannie turned around and looked at Jaewon solemnly.
Then, they felt a coolness upon the top of their left hand.
A painful small pinch followed, and Luannie recognized a
new, faint presence of something there. It was challenging to keep their face from distorting at the sensation.
"Yes. I need a moment," Luannie barely spoke through
still lips. "With Sebastian," they told her.

Sebastian looked between Luannie and Millie, ready to
leave the room.

"Okay... please come back inside soon to finish what you
miss from the video," Millie said.

Sebastian rose from his seat and followed Luannie as they
stormed through the open door of the technology room.
After pacing from one side of the lobby and back, Luannie
took a seat on the floor, and Sebastian accompanied them.

"Sebastian. Jaewon and I are seeing things that aren't
here. No amount of homesickness explains that," Luannie
told him. "Jaewon isn't seeing his father, and I didn't just
see my brother in there. How is this happening?" Luannie looked up and took a good look at Sebastian's face,
something they hadn't had the chance to do before. They
noticed a mole near his nose and how his eyebrows had a
naturally arched shape. "Have you or Samara experienced
anything unusual?"

Sebastian eyed the television where a different news segment was showing than before, and it was about the record-high levels of tourists in Sweden. "Not really," he answered before looking back to Luannie. "But I can only speak for myself."

"Well, don't you think it's strange?" Luannie asked with urgency, irritated that Sebastian did not seem as concerned as they were. He was about to speak, but they continued, "Jaewon says he saw his father again while we were walking here, that he didn't trip over some plant." They ran their hand through their long, wavy hair. "What if something happens to me?"

"Like what?" Sebastian asked.

"Like seeing my brother again," they said, leaving out the feelings they felt in their hand earlier. Luannie watched the door to the technology room slide down but didn't have time to mention it because the next thing they saw was Nathaniel returning to campus through the windows of the waiting room, trying to cross the street. Luannie pivoted to face Sebastian. "Are you going to get one of those chips?" they asked hurriedly.

He turned over his palms. "I don't see why not, and we won't have it forever. As Millie said, they're to get around easily, and I think it's kind of cool."

Nathaniel entered the building with several tote bags dangling from his arms and stopped in his tracks. "Why,

hello, you two! What are you doing sitting on the floor?"
His eyes searched the room for the others. "Alone?"

Luannie rose. "Just talking over some things before we
decide whether or not to get the microchip."

"Same here," Sebastian said in agreement as he also got
up to his feet.

"Millie should be going over everything with you all. It's
great news that you'll have them, especially since you'll
need to get in and out of this place!" Nathaniel lifted his
arms out in front of him for them to see the tote bags
he was carrying and explained, "I had to go run a quick
errand since we promised you lunch and, well, forgot I
had offered to pick it up!"

Luannie relaxed at the thought of having lunch. "Let us
help you," they said calmly, grabbing the handles of a few
bags. Sebastian walked over to help as well.

Nathaniel swiped his hand, which raised the door to the
technology room, and motioned for the two of them to
walk through.

"Oh, welcome back, you two—three!" Millie said as she
walked over.

A tall, beautiful woman with long braided hair was in
the room, now putting a transparent bandage over Jaewon's hand.

"I'd like for you two to meet Nova. She just finished placing a chip for Jaewon," Millie said.

"It didn't hurt much," Jaewon exclaimed enthusiastically with the same energy Luannie remembered from when they first met. It made them happy. "Are you both all right?" he asked them.

"Yeah, we're fine," Sebastian answered.

Nathaniel lifted the tote bags in his hands. "We'll set these down until everyone is ready."

As Millie reset the video to the beginning, Luannie noticed Nova's glance. They nodded at her, and Nova returned a graceful nod.

"Hello, you two," she said as she removed her gloves. "I hear you are the first students to join this new program, and I'm sure your advisors can expect great things from you throughout the year. You may call me Nova. I am a superintendent, engineer, and microchip placer from Chipd. Ask me any questions you have."

The tone of her voice enamored Luannie.

"Please, watch the rest of our short presentation, and afterward, Millie will be happy to go over the release forms with you in further detail," Nova said.

Luannie and Sebastian took their seats, but neither was paying attention to the presentation. Luannie noticed Sebastian eyeing Nathaniel as he walked over to where Millie was helping Samara with her tablet. Luannie began observing Nova as she spoke with Jaewon about his new microchip.

The video started from the beginning, but it didn't include the scene with Koa that Luannie remembered.

Once it was over, Millie gave each of them a tablet and rushed through the content of the forms. "Is there anything else we haven't covered that you two have any questions about?"

"Does it hurt?" Sebastian asked Millie.

"Just a pinch," Nova answered, hovering an index finger over her thumb.

After Sebastian and Luannie finished signing their forms, Nova hooked Sebastian's left arm into his chair strap. As she used a tool to carefully place the microchip onto an instrument, Luannie watched Jaewon and Samara stealing bits of their lunches already with Nathaniel. "Shortly," Nova said without any context. Sebastian and Luannie waited for her to say more, but she focused on cleaning Sebastian's hand. Nova instructed Sebastian to take a deep breath and said, "Then you two can eat," as she placed his microchip. He didn't even flinch.

Luannie waited in their chair as Nova quietly cleaned her tools in preparation for their microchip placement next. Luannie was not one to make small talk, so instead, they observed Millie scanning through the scholars' release forms, making sure everyone had signed legibly and where they were supposed to. Millie must have felt Luannie's eyes because she looked sideways for a moment before walking away. Luannie's gaze wandered over to Nathaniel, who was laughing because Sebastian pointed out a few crumbs that had fallen onto the floor. Luannie quickly sat upright as the cold from the disinfectant wiped over their hand. They were now more aware of Nova's presence as she instructed them to take a deep breath.

What if I start bleeding? What if she makes a mistake? What will my family think? What would my friends back in Niue think?

"Just a pinch," Nova reminded them softly.

Luannie sealed their eyes shut and ground their teeth in anticipation of the pain. A sharp sting made them shiver, and the feeling of a thin, long device reached a little deeper in their hand, omitting a small object. The piece remained in their skin, and the device took its time sliding out of their flesh. It reminded Luannie of the sensation they felt after seeing Koa on screen earlier. When Luannie opened their eyes, there were spots of light from having squeezed them shut so tightly.

Nova patted on the transparent tape she applied to their hand. "Phenomenal," she whispered with a delayed wink.

"If you've noticed, there are doors on every wall in this room." Nathaniel pointed around the lobby. Luannie didn't know what Nathaniel meant by that because all they could see was the front door, an elevator on the back wall, and the entrance to the technology room.

He scanned his left hand over the elevator button, and the door raised into the wall, revealing the elevator's interior. He looked at the scholars with the look of a child at a show and tell. "We will only be using the three doors in this room that you've used today, although there is another just beside the television. You won't be needing to use that door during your time here." Nathaniel scanned his hand to close the elevator and pointed directly at Sebastian. "You. Why don't you test out your microchip by opening the elevator? Nova preprogrammed them with access to the locks."

Sebastian finally looked something other than chill; he looked excited and even honored, perhaps. He waved his left hand to unlock the door and immediately stepped onto the platform of the elevator.

"Oh, wait!" Nathaniel said, but it was too late. Sebastian bent his knees as the elevator rose and the door shut closed simultaneously.

The scholars looked to Nathaniel. "And then there were three!" he laughed. "But seriously, when you open the door, don't do what he did. You're not supposed to step right on. First, there is a side panel with buttons for you to press. You can select how many people will be stepping on and what floor you'd like to go to, and it can travel horizontally on the second floor. If you don't indicate anything, it takes you straight up to the roof."

He looked around at the scholars, and they all looked back at him incredulously.

"Right, so... I'm sure Sebastian is rather confused at this time. Why don't you all head up there?"

Jaewon stepped up to open the door with his chip and walked onto the platform, followed by Luannie and Samara.

"Don't spend all your time up there! Once Millie is finished wrapping up with Nova, she will be waiting in the lobby to walk you over to the Uppsala Cathedral. Should you need anything at all, contact one of us through the School of IR app on your phone." With a shake of his phone, Nathaniel turned to exit the building. The front door of the building closed behind him as the elevator door shut in front of the three scholars.

The elevator walls were transparent from the inside out, so Luannie could catch quick glimpses of the second floor as the platform shot them up onto the roof. On the second floor, directly above the first-floor lobby, an enclosed hall seemed to connect both sides of the room. Luannie couldn't see any lockers or vending machines, but the elevator moved too quickly to spot much of anything. The elevator platform came to a stop, the door rose, and there was Sebastian, sitting with his long legs dangling from the edge, taking in the view.

Without speaking, Luannie, Jaewon, and Samara dispersed to see the city from different viewpoints. They weren't far from the Uppsala Cathedral, and Luannie could see it standing tall and red about six blocks in the distance. They could also make out the main building of Uppsala University. The sun was beginning to beam on their forehead, a feeling they had missed since leaving Hawaii.

Clank! The elevator door, which had been sticking straight into the air, lowered over the opening to the elevator. It seemed efficient when the doors ascended into the walls in the lobby, but sticking out into mid-air on the rooftop seemed unnecessary.

Luannie walked over to where Sebastian was gazing off, seemingly without intent. "Did you even try to go back down?"

He shook his head. "Nah." Then he slapped the concrete beside him, and Luannie took a seat. He slowly stuck out his hand without pointing and said, "There it is."

They followed his eye line to see what he was referencing. "Are you excited to see it? I've seen photos; the interior design is amazing."

"Nope." The right profile of Sebastian's face turned to Luannie, his eyebrow dipping to protect his eye from the glare of the sun. "But I'm sure it's stunning." They smirked and got more comfortable on the ledge beside him. "It's no ocean, but this is a nice view. *Ah!*"

Luannie jumped, startled. "Jaewon!"

"Just wanted to scare you," he said, taking a seat by Luannie, and Samara took a seat on the opposite side of

Jaewon. The scholars sat in the same order as they did in the technology room. "So, are we going to check out the second floor on the way back down, or should we meet with Millie first?"

The scholars answered him in shrugs, all too preoccupied with appreciating the scenery. Luannie guessed this suburban setting was something new for the other scholars as well. A timeless five minutes went by with no sounds heard, and it reminded Luannie of sitting on the beach with Koa, enjoying the serenity of the wind and solitude from the city. But with the thought of Koa, they opened their eyes and analyzed the side of their left hand.

"It's pretty cool, right?" Samara said.

"Yeah," Luannie managed to say. Samara was leaning forward, smirking at them. Luannie started to smile but quickly erased it. "I mean... I'm not sure."

"Should we get going?" Jaewon suggested, now positioned upright with attentive eyes. "Let's go back inside," he said hastily, breathing faster than usual.

Luannie gave him a nudge. "Yes, we can go back inside. No problem."

Jaewon closed his eyes and began to sway as if he was about to faint. His face was pulling forward as though he couldn't keep it above his neck.

"Hey," Luannie said, steadying his shoulders.

"I need to get down," Jaewon cried, tears peeking through tightened eyes.

Sebastian was already there, prepared to help him up to his feet.

"Are you afraid of heights?" Samara inquired.

Sebastian led Jaewon away from the ledge to return to the elevator.

Despite Sebastian's support, Jaewon's balance seemed to worsen, his body wobbling side to side. Luannie watched him duck out from underneath Sebastian's arm, turn around, and they observed in silent curiosity as Jaewon took a step, step, step, fall. A fall right off the ledge of the two-story roof on which they had sat.

A beat of nothing permeated through the air among the scholars in his sudden absence. Then, Sebastian bolted toward the elevator, Luannie ran to lean over the ledge, and Samara drifted backward in a state of shock.

"Jaewon!" Luannie called after him, but Sebastian called for the two of them.

"Come on!"

Luannie grabbed a stunned Samara by the arm and ran to meet Sebastian in time for the elevator. *What the hell is going on? Why would Jaewon do that?* they thought, baffled.

CHAPTER X

Distant mumbles grew louder until words became decipherable. Jaewon's eyelids parted, and faded silhouettes sharpened into nearby people.

"Is he?" a voice spoke.

"Maybe," a different voice responded.

"Hey, Millie!" the first voice shouted.

Wedges clattered along the floor from behind, then beneath, until they stopped in front of Jaewon on the bed. His bangs tickled his eyelashes, but he didn't move them out of his face. Cold knuckles tapped his forehead, and he realized he was staring sideways at long, white nails. The wedding band on the ring finger that sparkled in his eye had studs with a large silver diamond.

"Jaewon?"

He heard Millie and said nothing as a blanket dragged along his side and tucked around his neck. The memory foam medical bed he was sunken into felt familiar. He was so still that he was unable to decipher where his body lay and the mattress began. His pupils rolled to the corners of his eyes toward where three people leaned against the wall. One person was sitting on the floor in front of him. Leading with his chest, Jaewon tried lifting himself.

"Hey, how are you feeling?" It was Aria from her seat on the floor. She grasped onto the bottom of her shirt, lightly wrinkled from having twisted on it periodically out of nerves.

Various sources of pain increased in intensity as Jaewon bent his legs, and he sank back into the bed. *Ach!* Discomfort shot from the top of his right foot, through his ankle and kneecap, and up to his waist. It felt as though he had forcefully created new limbs, and the pins and needle tingling spread all over.

"Jaewon, try not to move so much," Millie advised. "It's okay to relax where you are."

His elbows were propping up his upper body now, and he faced the wall. Sebastian, Samara, and Luannie were observing him, the corners of all their mouths curved downward. "Hi," Jaewon said dryly with a weak smile.

Luannie pouted. "How do you feel?"

He whipped his hair to the side out of habit and immediately felt a muscle strain in his neck. He winced and sucked in a breath through his teeth. "Good, good. Are we in the medical room?"

"Yeah," Sebastian answered while squeezing one of the stress relief balls in his palm.

There was quiet as Aria rose from the floor. She and Millie exchanged hushed words before Millie left the room, and the ring of the elevator button sounded through the housing hall.

"We missed you this morning," Jaewon told Aria.

"Oh." She let out a giggle. "You're so sweet." Her eyes searched his face, where a few specks of dry blood remained after a prior nose bleed. "Are you in any pain?" she asked, to which he nodded. "Well, I can have Millie increase your dose of pain reliever when she returns."

Jaewon shut his eyes until they watered. It felt similar to the burn that occurs when finally blinking again over dry eyes.

"I'm not suicidal," he whispered, somehow grabbing even more attention from everyone in the room than was already on him. "I didn't jump off the roof."

"Jaewon—" Luannie began.

"I know, but I didn't walk off that roof."

Luannie squinted and turned their face away from him. *I watched you, and I watched you walk right past me,* they reminded themself.

Jaewon could see Luannie's frown trembling and eyelids fluttering rapidly.

"We're glad you're going to be okay," Samara said on a lighter note.

"Yeah, we've been scared shitless for you," Sebastian told him, impassioned.

Shortly after the elevator rang, Millie came walking back into the room with Nathaniel behind her. He spread his palms over the bed beside Jaewon's knees to make space for himself to take a seat.

"Oh," Nathaniel sighed, nearly in a whine. "You frightened us all." He tilted his head like that of a curious puppy. "That was quite a fall you had. You're fortunate to be awake right now with only a few broken bones and bruises. If you hadn't fallen on the bushes lining the campus building, things might have happened differently." He winked at Jaewon and took a look down at his leg. "You've been in here for about five hours now, healing under our supervision. Jaewon, would you like to spend the night here? If you decide to stay, we'll be able to check in on you," Nathaniel offered. "If not, we can try to move you into your room, but it may not be best considering how sore you are."

"Thanks. I think I want to sleep in my room tonight," Jaewon decided.

Nathaniel nodded slowly in hesitant approval. "Then you shall." Nathaniel paused before continuing. "Also… we think that speaking with Aria sometime tomorrow about how you're feeling would be a good idea. Aria is a great help! If there's anyone you can go to for something, it's her," he said, drawing a pink blush from Aria's cheeks and a quick glare from Millie's polar ice blue eyes.

"Sure. I'd love to," Jaewon responded. He lightly wiggled the toes in his right foot. "Are you sure I'm going to be all right?" He became aware that his leg did not move as quickly upon command as it had once before, and he was concerned about what might have happened to him. He examined the lower half of his body as though it were separate from himself.

Millie responded, "Your right foot and leg broke, and you've likely bruised several ribs as well." She waited a moment for Jaewon to digest the information before reassuring him, "You'll be all right. Your casts will stay on for a few weeks, and we have already prepared a pair of crutches to match your height so that you can walk short distances if needed. But it may take up to a full two months before you feel confident walking on it again with your full body weight. Jaewon," her tone changed, "you are *very* fortunate to have sustained minor injuries, considering the circumstances. You could have punctured a lung or fractured your skull, and not many people live to say they survived a second-story fall onto a concrete sidewalk." Her eyes looked straight through his as if she could see his brain, and he felt frozen.

"Yeah, I know." To avoid his low-spoken response from being mistaken for disappointment, he added, "I'm thankful."

"He's in an awful lot of pain still. Can we raise his dose?" Aria requested Millie.

"Certainly," Nathaniel answered after Millie provided no immediate response.

"Jaewon, tell us how do you feel right now? Do you feel like you might be able to get out of the bed with our help and use these crutches to head into your room? We think you should consider how it may be easier for you to spend the night in here," Millie asked Jaewon.

He smiled at the other scholars. "If they come with me to my room, I'll be fine."

"Great!" Nathaniel exclaimed, getting off of the bed. "Millie and I will help you sit up and walk to your room." He addressed the other scholars. "And if you will be accompanying him, maybe see to it that he has something small to eat and drink tonight?"

It took about five minutes for Millie and Nathaniel to get Jaewon up onto his left foot while he held steadily onto his crutches. They walked alongside him to the front door of his room and opened it for him using the key from his School of International Relations tote bag. From there, it took another five minutes to get him situated comfortably into his bed. After Nathaniel assured Jaewon that he could reach out at any time should he find himself needing help, Nathaniel and Millie exited his room to adjourn with Aria in the hall, and the three scholars entered cautiously.

"Hey, you," said Sebastian, dragging out the words. "It's nice to see you awake again."

Jaewon peered at the medicine Millie left on the side table for him with a scrunched nose. "I guess I have to take that."

"We'll help," Samara offered. "Is it all right if we sit on the floor in here for a bit? We'd like to spend some time with you—if you're not too tired."

"Tired? I just slept the whole day away; I think I'll be up for a while," he told her jokingly. "I don't mind if you all stay for a bit; that'd be nice. I'll probably need to sleep again in another hour." Jaewon reached over to take his anti-epileptic medication since he realized he missed his midday dose. Feeling the weight of the silence in the room, he said, "So, it looks like Jaewon is zero to two on group excursions so far, huh?"

Luannie giggled at his use of the third person. "No... 'Jaewon' didn't miss anything today, and neither did we. If anything, we missed you. It was a unanimous decision not to go to the Uppsala Cathedral. We've all been worried sick and waiting for you to wake back up."

"You know how to scare people, huh?" Sebastian commented with a wink.

"Did you end up checking out the second floor? What does it look like?" Jaewon asked.

Puzzled by his question, Samara said, "We came straight downstairs to take care of you."

"We were all so worried on our way down from the roof. We weren't sure how we were going to find you. You were unresponsive for a long time." Luannie leaned back to take a breath and bit on their lip. "I ran back inside to get Millie and Nova, and then they called Nathaniel. We were all there for you."

Jaewon thought about how anytime he would have an episode back home, his father, if around, didn't know what to do. It was always his mother who had to care for him. Now, he was with new people in another country, and people were still finding themselves in situations where they needed to take care of him. Jaewon elongated his face as he tried to prevent himself from sobbing.

"We're thrilled that you're all right," Luannie told him. "I just... I didn't know what you were doing when you turned around up there. If I had known that would happen, I wouldn't have just let you do that. I thought you were going to look at something or…" Their voice cracked, and Sebastian tapped a supportive knuckle on their shoulder. Luannie had their hair pulled up into a bun now, and they fidgeted awkwardly with their hands without having their hair dangling down with which to play.

"Please don't feel guilty. None of this is any of your fault," Jaewon said. He gulped and peered through the window, out at the magenta sky. "Something came over me, and I've never felt compelled to do anything as dangerous as that, and I didn't want to as I was doing it, either."

"Then why did you?" Samara asked, and everyone looked toward Jaewon for an explanation.

"I didn't. My head wasn't in control of my body. I just watched myself in silence as I approached the edge and took that final step." He looked at them with sincerity. "I was scared half to death by what was happening. But it wasn't my idea to do that." His words softened to nothing at the end of his last sentence because he noticed how absurd he sounded.

Nobody said anything until Samara stood up and prepared Jaewon's medicine for him according to the instructions left by Millie. "It says here that you'll take this medicine tonight and again in the morning."

"I still think he should have stayed in the hospital," Luannie muttered.

"I was in the hospital?" Jaewon asked, his head lifting slightly off his pillow as Samara rose the medicine cup to his mouth.

"Don't you know? Millie is a teacher, a program director, *and* a medical professional," Sebastian said sarcastically. "You could have stayed in the hospital longer, but the doctors wanted to run a few more X-rays on the upper half of your body and to check for a concussion. However, Millie thought it was 'excessive.'"

Jaewon scrunched his face with the taste of the remaining sour flavor from the medicine in his mouth.

"I think it'd be a good idea for us all to write down some local emergency contact information," Luannie thought aloud. "In case we ever need it."

Samara took a seat by Luannie and Sebastian on the floor.

"Can someone say something about themselves now?" Jaewon pleaded. "Anything. I just want to get to know you all more. I missed out on an opportunity in Stockholm yesterday, and then I ruined another opportunity for us to bond at the cathedral today. We didn't even get to see the rest of our 'campus.' Let's talk about something else for a while."

"You didn't ruin a thing, Jaewon," Sebastian said. "Let's see... Well, I've already shared that I played varsity soccer in high school. I guess it's also important for you to know that I greatly value friendship," he said with a hand placed over his chest, making eye contact with Jaewon. "That's all for me tonight. Who's turn next?"

"Well, hold on now," Jaewon said. "This is the first time I've ever had a varsity athlete in my room. I'd like to take this moment to appreciate the full circle I've gone through. I think this makes me popular."

The scholars laughed, inspired by his humor while in his present circumstance.

Sebastian asked, "How about you, Samara? Anything about yourself you feel like sharing with the rest of us?"

She looked to her right and touched her chin like a cartoon character would to indicate they were thinking. "Hmm," she slumped. "I'd like to follow in my mother's footsteps someday. She goes on a lot of business trips in Europe. She was actually in Sweden recently. Although, if I had a job like that, I would choose not to have kids." Samara noticed the others were all focusing on her, and she recoiled a bit. "I had a tutor growing up," Samara changed the topic. "She taught me Chinese, English, and a little Navajo."

"Navajo?" Luannie asked, intrigued. "That's awesome. I'd like to learn Navajo too."

Samara smiled in acknowledgment before continuing. "I love learning new languages, and I also like to cook. I don't mind making something for you to eat tonight, Jaewon," Samara offered. "You must be hungry, and I can make you some balaleet."

"Some... what?" Jaewon asked.

Samara laughed, "It's fried noodles with spices topped with an omelet and some nuts; you have to try it."

Jaewon could tell how excited Samara seemed and didn't want to turn down her favor. "Sure, I could go for some balala..."

"Balaleet," she enunciated. "I'll make it soon, but first, I want to hear you and Luannie tell us a little something about yourselves." She looked between the two of them, waiting to see who would share first.

Jaewon motioned his head toward Luannie, and they started undoing the bun in their hair, which they had put up at the hospital earlier.

"Uhm... I had a close friend when I still lived in Niue. They were also 'third gender,' as many on our island. I miss them very much, but we don't talk anymore. We also made jewelry together with my parents," they reminisced. "Like the piece I made that's hanging around Jaewon's neck!"

He smiled and grabbed onto the necklace they had given him, relieved it was still intact after the day's events.

"That looks nice!" Sebastian said.

"Thanks. I'd made them all the time with my parents growing up. Now I have Koa. I hope my parents are taking good care of him." They ran their fingers through the curtain of hair that hung from the side of their head. "I'm sure they are," they tried to convince themself.

Jaewon thought back on his life to determine if he could find anything worth sharing. *I listen to opera on occasion because it gives me the chills.* "I didn't tell my mother that my father was having an affair right away," he found himself saying instead. "Eh…" He refused to move his eyes from where he glued them to the ceiling. *Why the hell did I tell them that of all things?* "I used to have a pen pal from the United States, but he was kind of racist."

Sebastian slanted his neck. "Affair? Kind of racist?"

"Mhmm," Jaewon continued in response to both questions. "I don't want to get into all that, though." He didn't see, but the scholars exchanged confused expressions. "Oh! And I've always wanted to travel outside of Seoul, and my mom and I plan to travel to Pyeongchang county when I go back home."

"I remember you were telling me about that," Samara recalled. "South Korea sounds like a nice place." And with that, she exited the room to start cooking.

Jaewon beamed. He wasn't used to having many friends to speak with, let alone any who remembered their previous conversations together. And he knew Samara was right. South Korea is an excellent place with so much more for him to explore. He became lost in thought about the future of this program and missed Samara's exit to prepare his dinner.

"Luannie, what happened earlier?" Jaewon implored. "You left during the microchip presentation. Are you feeling better about everything now?"

"Something happened I can't quite explain." They checked the door as if to make sure nobody could overhear. "It's odd that you've been seeing your father, and during that video, I swore I saw my brother."

Jaewon's lips parted, wanting to say something but wanting to hear more.

"So, you're not alone in feeling like there's something wrong with you. Sebastian…" Luannie said in a high voice and waited for him to start speaking.

Sebastian shuffled on the floor and stretched out his back. "Neither of you is alone, and it looks like we've all been going through something lately."

Jaewon frowned, staring at Sebastian. *Well, don't leave me in suspense now.*

"All of us were keeping you company in the medical room earlier today when I started seeing and feeling things. I pulled Luannie into the hall to get away from the others and just…" He widened his eyes, attempting to keep the water in his tear duct. "I broke down. The pain was excruciating, and I felt like I was on fire."

Luannie draped their right arm across his shoulder, and Jaewon had to fight the envy and listen to Sebastian's memory.

"Holes were burning into my palms, my feet. Then, I felt fingertips make the shape of an upside-down cross, stopping at my forehead. I was so confused," his voice broke.

Jaewon had never seen Sebastian this vulnerable and seeing his friend hurt angered him.

"And the idea of it all was uncomfortable, but after a minute, I told myself that it wasn't real." Sebastian leaned his head into his palm, with his elbow digging into his leg. "I knew because Luannie couldn't realize anything physically wrong was occurring to me. The whole experience was exhausting, and then I had to go back into that room like nothing ever happened."

The silence was loud.

After some time passed, Jaewon pulled on a chain to close his window blinds. *I wonder if Samara has something to share with us too.*

Knock knock.

Jaewon, startled, jerked forward and immediately regretted doing so. His usually full lips were now thin and surrounding two rows of clenched teeth as he waited for the pain in his right leg to subside. He patted his cast lightly and looked toward the door of his room.

Knock knock knock knock.

Sebastian looked sideways at Jaewon from the spot on the floor where he had fallen asleep. He squiggled the arm bent beneath his neck and then used it as a platform under his side.

Lying there in that position, Jaewon couldn't help but picture Sebastian as a mermaid, and he chuckled at the image in his head.

"Just a second!" Sebastian called, anticipating another round of knocks. He dragged himself along the floor to open the door, and there stood Samara, a dish in her hands. A wave of sweet and spice rushed into the small room.

"I made you some—" Samara started speaking excitedly before noticing Luannie still sleeping on the floor. Their hair swirled around their face as though they had purposefully placed it there. "Balaleet," Samara whispered and tiptoed over to Jaewon's side.

Sebastian stood up with his hands on his hips. "I can't believe we fell asleep."

"It took me about an hour to make this, so it should be around nine now," Samara said as she rested the dish on Jaewon's chest.

His eyes darted to Samara's and then to the space around her until he realized she would only look away once he tried her food. Jaewon prepared himself to convey an impressed expression no matter how it tasted, but he didn't have to pretend. "Oh, wow," he said, balaleet still in his mouth. "This is good," he said while chewing and shoveling in another fork-full.

"Take a breath," Sebastian teased.

"Samara," Jaewon said, and she laughed. He was incoherent—barely audible. He lifted a finger to indicate a pause and then hovered it in the air over his mouth until it was empty. "When did you get your microchip?"

Samara's face froze, and she watched Jaewon look at her. "It was the first thing I wanted to do when I got here."

Jaewon jutted his chin outward and pressed his lips together. "Was that the first thing you did after Nathaniel picked you up from the airport?" He looked up at her, but she was quiet. He could feel the pressure of Sebastian's glare and began to wonder if his questions came off too strongly. Jaewon lifted his eyelids a bit more and gave a small smile.

"After establishing myself in my room, I searched for the nearest public microchip placement site and headed down. The placer only asked for my documents to verify my identity and was able to insert it right then since I'm a temporary resident," she explained quickly and let out a huff of air. "Take your time eating that. I can come back for the dish sometime tomorrow." Samara tiptoed over Luannie and whispered, "Take care," to the boys before exiting the room.

Jaewon shrugged at Sebastian. Then, he could see that Luannie's eyes were open as they lay on the floor.

"Is someone awake?" Jaewon asked playfully.

Their eyes moved drowsily in his direction, and they stated, "She's full of shit."

CHAPTER XI

Six in the morning. Light peeked in through the window behind the hanging blind, and Jaewon pulled it back to take a look outside. The city of Uppsala appeared muted, faint, and he desired to move as quietly as the streets were at this time.

He grabbed his crutches that were leaning against the nightstand. He winced as he swung himself sideways on the bed and struggled to stand on his left foot. Hoping not to disturb Samara or Luannie, whose rooms were on either side of his, he slipped a comfortable sneaker onto his left foot. Jaewon prevented himself from scratching at the itches inside his cast by kicking it gently out in front of him.

The hall was barren as he took his time swinging to the elevator. Sebastian's room, located on the other side of Luannie's, was the farthest, and Samara's the closest. Sounds of metal clinking from the medical room as he passed stopped him in his tracks. The elevator was not much further, but Jaewon couldn't help but wonder who was in there. He leaned against the wall beside the door to the medical room and listened closely.

"...exactly what I thought would happen," he heard a woman say. "Not to mention... Yes, they're brilliant." It wasn't easy to make out the words because the woman was moving around the room. It was quiet for a few seconds before the woman spoke on just the opposite side of the door. "Then I'd better start heading out," she said clearly.

Jaewon panicked, gathered strength in his shoulders, and raced to the elevator, which let out a loud ring upon pressing the button. He hurriedly shuffled in when the medical room door opened. He slammed on the button multiple times, and the elevator door had nearly closed as he saw Millie wave to him and say, "Good morning." The door slid shut, and he was left alone in the elevator as it descended.

Jaewon waited in the housing building lobby for Millie to come down to give her an explanation; otherwise, she may follow after him. The receptionist didn't say anything to him, and after waiting a minute, he used a crutch as an arm to open the front door and began swinging down the street.

He passed where Nathaniel had spoken with the scholars the morning before, and he saw the top of the Uppsala Cathedral in the distance. By the time he had made it to the third block, his arm muscles were already exhausted, and his right knee ached.

"Hey, look at you," a man called out to Jaewon from inside one of the street cafés. "Aren't you that kid who fell yesterday? What are you doing walking around?"

Jaewon recognized the man walking toward him as one of the bystanders who had seen him when he fell yesterday, seemingly over a potted plant. He'd forgotten to answer the man as he glared at the plant now, resting against a window.

"Are you feeling all right? How about a cup of coffee, free of charge," the man offered.

Jaewon analyzed the café owner's colorful apron over his moderately extended stomach. He couldn't have been more than thirty-one years old, and he was rather handsome.

Jaewon smiled and said, "No, thanks. Just make sure your plants don't wander too far away." He couldn't see behind him, but the café owner smirked and bent down to organize the plants in the outdoor dining area.

After a couple of blocks more, Jaewon stopped in front of the tan-brown brick building that he called "campus" and stared at the ground before him. He tried to imagine the scene of him falling from the height of a two-story building's roof and then remembered what Millie had told him about his fortune. *You're fortunate to be awake right now with only a few broken bones and bruises*, is what she had said.

Jaewon didn't believe in fortune, but he acknowledged that his survival was astonishing.

You fell two stories, and all you suffered are a few broken bones. That is unbelievable.

Jaewon tried to make out a view of the housing building in the distance. He figured it would be at least three hours more until the other scholars woke up. Then, the thought of Millie or anyone else searching for him popped into his mind and became daunting. The campus building before him appeared taller, felt taller than usual now as he vertically extended his neck, unable to identify the end of the building's height. Although he knew it was still only two stories, it grew increasingly high, feeling more like a tower with no top in his sight. A gravitational pull instilled into Jaewon an instinctual urge to be on top of that roof at a higher elevation. And he would not feel satisfied until his legs were dangling once again from the ledge where he'd sat the day before.

Looking back down the blocks leading from where the other scholars slept, he discreetly opened the front door and walked inside toward the elevator straight across the lobby.

Skid, halt.

His feet stopped moving midway through the room, and he rotated to face the wall on his right. The television had turned on, and a man from the Swedish Armed

Forces was in the middle of broadcasting a public service announcement.

"He is survived by his fathers, Oliver and Elias Rozelle. His coworkers at Chipd describe him as one of the most eager, communicative, and brilliant employees to have made an early mark at the company. Mattias had most recently been preparing to work under one Superintendent Nova on her new project to create the first high-intelligence brain microchip. It was said by the superintendent previously today that Mattias was certainly the most dedicated junior with which she has had the pleasure of working. Along with the news of the sudden passing of Chipd employee Mattias Rozelle comes a special message concerning—"

Zap! The television abruptly shut off, and Jaewon's feet marched again in the direction of the elevator.

Desire is a word meant for strong people, he heard a voice tell himself. *The desire to be, the desire to do. Are your desires strong? Are you strong enough for them, against them?*

He swiped his hand and stepped onto the elevator's platform, as if on auto-pilot, and allowed the elevator to lift him onto the roof. Jaewon then watched ahead as the door to the elevator raised, jutting into the sky, and the pink of morning incrementally entered the elevator until flooding over him.

Incredulously, he began to identify visions of Pyeongchang County in his surroundings. A chilly fog entered his view that mischievously blended in with Uppsala's small buildings and streets. He tightened his grasp on what once were his crutches but now were skis—and meshed into the sky before Jaewon were mountains now, their snow-covered peaks casting shadows on the peaks behind them. He swung his way off the elevator, and the door vanished from behind him.

Jaewon looked back out toward the ledge of the roof, but it was no longer there. He stood feebly on a small mountain covered in snow and could feel the icy water seeping into his cast. Uppsala had converted into the great outdoors with no end to the mountaintop peaks around him in his sight. As he rolled his neck, trying to ignore the pain pulsating in his leg, only one structure stood tall in the distance: the housing building. Jaewon couldn't comprehend how it was level to where he stood since the campus building was shorter than the housing building, but he didn't panic. Nothing about this change of scenery panicked him because the soothing tone of a familiar voice gradually eased him into believing. "Everything is okay. I'm here. You're going to be all right," his mother spoke to him in Korean before gliding past him on the mountain, flashing a smile and letting out a celebratory laugh before heading down the slope in front of them. "Join me, Jaewon!" she yelled.

Jaewon swung himself forward to see her ski down the mountain he stood on, but a looming feeling stole his attention and diverted it to the roof of the housing building. So far away, and yet he could recognize a person's silhouette. He swung himself forward a bit more, allowing his skis to help him travel. *Is that him? No.*

Jaewon felt as weak as he had the day he received acceptance into the School of International Relations. He pictured himself at his kitchen table, his father walking back up the stairs to see him on the floor before turning around to go back down the stairs. And his mother, never so livid, slammed her knees onto the kitchen floor to kneel beside him. He remembered her embrace as she had positioned him upright and assured him that he would be fine while picking bits of glass out of his forearm. He wanted to be with her now, to meet her at the bottom of the slope before him.

The orange glow of the sun weighed on his eyelids, and he opened them slowly to find that the roof to the housing building was closer now. The silhouette and its features were clearly defined. His skis slid steadily beneath him through the snow as he stared into the man's face. His mind and heart began to race, blood pumping forcefully in his chest, and a chill ran up his spine. Jaewon watched the silhouette of his father turn away and vanish along with the housing building. Only mountains surrounded him now.

The ground had unwillingly moved out from underneath Jaewon, steepening the slope of the mountain on which he had stood. Suddenly, he saw the sun whip in and out of view and felt the wind tickle the skin of his palms. Everything was spinning and rapidly decreasing in elevation, and he knew he would see his mother soon. *Unbelievable.*

"Hu!" Luannie was startled awake.

CHAPTER XII

They swore they had experienced a plunging sensation. *It was only the jerks,* Luannie told themself as they steadied their chopped breaths, preparing to return to sleep. *It was only a dream.* A split second in time flashed before their eyes: the bird's-eye perspective of plummeting toward a concrete sidewalk and with it, the transfer of a feeling that turned their gut nauseous and prompted them to run to Sebastian's door.

Sebastian grumbled, waving away his father's applause. He visited a soccer field with his father at his new job to watch a team practice. One of the players let Sebastian kick the ball, and after making a goal, his father clapped wildly. The applause grew slower and slower until it turned into knocking. He squeezed his eyes and tried to stop letting the thought of Samara waiting with her dish of balaleet on the other side of the door enter his dream. But the knocking persisted to the point that it scared him into awareness that somebody was there. Sebastian's eyes shot open. He jumped out of bed and to the door in only one leap.

Luannie was so frantic they accidentally knocked on Sebastian's chest before realizing he was standing in the doorway. They met eyes momentarily, and then Luannie walked forward, pushing him back into his room.

"Hey!" Sebastian exclaimed playfully. But seeing Luannie grasp nervously onto their horsetail of hair that was gathered together by a scrunchie, he figured it must be important.

Luannie held their inner wrists against their temples, applying pressure to calm themself down.

"What's going on?" Sebastian urged.

"I was asleep, I woke up, and I felt something," Luannie said before stopping to make sure Sebastian was paying attention. Then they rambled, "I felt so disgusted, like I was riding a rollercoaster without any kind of restraints. I wasn't in my room, though. I mean, I was laying down in my room, but I think—"

Sebastian raised a hand. "It's all right. Breathe. Did you have a nightmare?" he asked, still half-asleep.

"What?" Luannie responded breathlessly, whipping a warped face in his direction. "I'm twenty years old, Sebastian. I rarely get nightmares anymore."

He shrugged, grumbling in a hushed tone about a recent nightmare where he burned on a pew until he melted into a puddle, but Luannie didn't hear.

"It felt as though my whole body was there and then back in my bed." They demonstrated exaggeratedly with their hands. "I felt it!"

Sebastian put on a patient expression, and it was as though Luannie had heard his thought.

"I *know* this happened, and I need you to, please, listen to me," they implored.

"All right," he said in a high pitch, lifting his hands. "What do you want to do about your dream?"

"Well, I think what I saw was in front of campus."

"Wait," Sebastian dragged out slowly, an eyebrow perched. "So, you woke up because you felt something scary happen in front of campus? Luannie," he said calmly, lowering his head. "Don't you think…"

They bobbled their head side to side several times and interjected with, "No, no, I know what it seems like, but this isn't because of yesterday. I could physically feel the wind rushing past me." Luannie stopped to think about how absurd what they said had sounded.

Sebastian leaned back. He couldn't remember the last time he could recall a dream so vividly. "Okay, let's say this isn't a symptom of shock from what we went through yesterday. Did you want to go to campus and check it out? We can check out the second floor we never got to see, but we should probably invite Samara."

Luannie's eyes darted from Sebastian's sneakers to his unused School of International Relations tote bag and then to the necklace that hung around his neck.

Sebastian hovered his hand over his mother's crystal but withdrew when he noticed Luannie was also wearing a necklace, which reminded him of the one they had given Jaewon. He reluctantly put on his shoes and, with an extended arm, grabbed the tote bag up by its strap to use for the first time, as if he were changing a baby's diaper. Then he leaned it over his shoulder, hanging from his index and middle fingers, and popped a hip as if to say, "There, see? I'm finally using it." For a moment, it looked as if Luannie were going to smile, but they shot him a glare instead.

"Let's go now—the two of us," Luannie rushed Sebastian.

It was breezy outside, but the sun was warm enough that the chilly wind was bearable, a friendly welcome to the persistently hot weather. Seven-thirty in the morning looked ethereal, with light illuminating the outline of Uppsala's buildings.

The first couple of blocks that Luannie and Sebastian walked together had been secluded. Then, they approached people scattered along the sidewalk, all facing in the same direction. There was an ambulance and a familiar car parked across the street from the campus building. A tall man with windswept hair played charades with his arms during an intense conversation with medical personnel. Without needing to discuss, Luannie and Sebastian both quickened their pace to the scene. They crept to a stop among the crowd of people who had gathered around a sizable pool of blood.

"If you could just let me in, please! I don't have to ride with him; I need to see if that's one of my students in there!" Nathaniel begged through a scratchy throat. No other voices stood out, only indistinct chatter from onlookers who held tightly onto their coffee thermoses.

"Sir, again, I'm sorry, but we can't give you any personal information," a paramedic advised Nathaniel.

"Scan his hand microchip; if his name is Jaewon, then I know him!" Nathaniel's hands waved up and down as he spoke.

Luannie felt a sharp, hot pain shoot through their stomach. The whole scenario was too distressing to register fully at once, and the sound of Jaewon's name made them feel sick.

"We can't provide information to anyone besides family. Unless you are family, we won't be able to share anything at this time," the same paramedic responded, motioning for her colleague to climb into the ambulance.

It was early for so many people to be starting their day, but Luannie noticed the coffee thermoses people clutched onto were carved with the name of the café just down the block. A handsome man with an apron told one of the officers that he saw the boy fall while speaking with his customers outside the café.

"Just from the corner of my eye, and I couldn't believe it. I even talked to him this morning while he was swinging by on his crutches. He must've broken a foot or something. He did the same thing yesterday and landed in those bushes." The café owner pointed in the direction of the green bushes that lined the campus building. "I think this time… maybe he did it."

Luannie touched their fingers to Sebastian's wrist and backed away as the rest of the medical personnel stepped into the ambulance, and Nathaniel dashed to his car. They both walked to the café's outdoor dining area and sat in silence. Sebastian cried through strained muscles in a poor attempt to keep his face from drooping.

Luannie hadn't been sitting for long when they pulled their phone out of their tote bag and recorded a voice message on the School of IR app. "It's Luannie. Sebastian and I think Jaewon is seriously hurt. Something happened this morning, and we need to talk with you about it. Can you message me back when you're awake?" They sent the steadily paced audio message to Samara and then lifted the phone to their lips once again. "Hi, this is Luannie. Do you have time this morning to meet with Sebastian and me?" Their voice cracked, and they whispered, "It's important."

A little after eight o'clock, a small red car pulled in front of the café and opened its back door. The crowd down the street had dispersed, and customers who were somehow still hungry enough to stick around for breakfast surrounded Luannie and Sebastian. Luannie twiddled their fingers around in circles and avoided eye contact with the customers. They found the whiff of sweetness from the bakery nauseating and were glad when they climbed into the backseat of Aria's car.

Aria turned around to face Luannie and Sebastian in the backseat. The car freshener filled the car with the scent of cinnamon, and Luannie welcomed it, wanting nothing more at that moment than to smell something other than coffee. Aria appeared disheveled, wearing a thrown-on geometric T-shirt and black pants with silver rings around the thighs. She was about thirty-five, and her straight dark hair was thrown into a sunrise bun as her brown, nearly black eyes investigated Luannie's composure.

"Good morning," she greeted them cautiously. "I didn't realize you two were morning people." A song playing low on the radio sounded like a cross between techno, rock, and Frank Sinatra. Aria put the car into park and turned further around to better face them both than she was earlier. "Talk to me. What's going on?"

Sebastian's neck twisted as he observed the diners and realized that the street had cleared entirely from the chaos before.

Under Aria's patient gaze, Luannie said, "Jaewon fell."

"Oh, I know you must be worried about him, but I'm sure he's going to be all right—"

"No, he fell again this morning. He must've gone back to campus, and now he's in an ambulance on his way to the hospital," Sebastian stated with his forehead firmly planted against the window.

Aria looked as if she'd seen a ghost. "Are you sure?"

Luannie put on their seat belt and poked Sebastian, inviting him back into the conversation. "Nathaniel was here trying to get the paramedics to tell him who they had in the ambulance. But the owner of this café says it was the person who fell yesterday. He remembered Jaewon, and he even spoke with him this morning. We want to be anywhere else right now, please."

About forty minutes had passed since Luannie was feet away from a pool of blood on the sidewalk, and talking about the reality of the situation out loud now prompted an emotional response they could no longer suppress. Luannie's outburst of sobbing drew a gentle hug from Sebastian and a pair of enlarged, glassy eyes from Aria. It was now Luannie who faced away from the inside of the car as Sebastian sat upright. Aria pulled from the curve and drove to the nearby Linnaeus Garden, about ten minutes away.

As the car pulled into a parking spot, Aria excused herself for a moment while she contacted Nathaniel. She cleared her throat in preparation and even tightened the bun in her hair as if he'd be able to see her. "Nathaniel, I'm with Luannie and Sebastian now. They informed me—"

"Wait," Sebastian interrupted. "Can you not tell him we're with you, please?"

Luannie looked at him quizzically. *Why would you request that?*

Aria nodded and smiled warmly. "Sure," she said without further questioning, deleting her previous audio message. "Good morning, Nathaniel. Where are you now? I heard that Jaewon is," Aria pursed her lips, "seriously hurt at the moment. Could you please call me back or let me know how I can help?" She pressed send, let her hands fall awkwardly on her lap, and leaned against the steering wheel.

"Does Nathaniel usually go to the campus building this early?" Sebastian asked.

"Not that I know of, but he's always going in and out of there. Working on stuff and preparing things in that place for your first day of classes," Aria said. Silence followed and filled the car.

Luannie pictured the first time they had ever seen Nathaniel. He'd greeted them at the airport with his well-defined cheekbones and jawline, dark hair, striking emerald eyes that pierced straight through them, and his broad, flashy, radiant smile. They couldn't recall a set of teeth so white, especially none that contrasted against such pale skin.

"Were you with Jaewon this morning?" Aria asked in a sing-song tone that ended with a squeak. Luannie realized that while they were questioning Nathaniel, Aria was questioning the two of them.

"No. I'd speak more, but I need time to collect my thoughts," Luannie said.

"Aria, things haven't been feeling right with us," Sebastian explained. "You heard Jaewon in the medical room. He said he didn't walk off the roof yesterday, that he had no control over it. Plus, what happened with him during our trip to Stockholm? It adds up to something weird going on, and he isn't the only one who's been experiencing..."

Luannie didn't mind sharing with Aria what they saw happen to their brother in the technology room the other day. Still, perhaps Sebastian wasn't willing to share his own experiences, and they decided to keep theirs to themself.

Aria lightly tapped on the steering wheel and turned off the radio. "You two may already know that Jaewon has epilepsy. If he doesn't take his medicine regularly, he becomes prone to seizures and other behavior. But this doesn't rub off on other people by spending time together," Aria told them.

Sebastian made a noise as if he were about to interrupt, but he relaxed into his seat without offering his input.

"I was supposed to speak with him later today about how he's been doing. If I had any idea his thoughts were this serious, I wouldn't have left yesterday," Aria said.

Luannie leaned forward between the two front seats, and their head was almost beside Aria's shoulder. "You think Jaewon is suicidal?"

Aria took a deep inhale. "He jumped off of a roof. Maybe twice."

Luannie looked off, and their jaw opened at an angle when Aria's phone began ringing. Luannie retreated to their spot in the backseat with Sebastian and remained quiet, inpatient to hear what Nathaniel had to say.

"Nathaniel?"

"Aria, good morning. Yes, I am here at the hospital now. It's terrible. I was sitting in my car near campus when suddenly a crowd had formed by the front door. I went to check it out, and somebody was lying on the sidewalk, right next to where Jaewon fell yesterday. Oh..." Nathaniel sounded distraught. "Aria, it's terrible." He made a shivering sound and provided no further context.

"Do you know what happened? Do you have any information about his well-being?"

Luannie's stomach turned. *Please, please, please be okay. Please be okay with only another broken leg,* they thought repeatedly.

Nathaniel remained silent, and Luannie wiggled their head in disbelief, then again in anticipation.

"He succeeded this time," Nathaniel concluded breathily.

For the first time since picking up Sebastian and Luannie from the café, Aria cried.

"I just updated Millie, and she'll be in touch with you shortly. Ugh." Nathaniel groaned.

Luannie couldn't determine whether to fight their urge to sympathize with Nathaniel or to grill him on all of the uncertainties running through their head.

"Let me call you back later, all right? A lot is going on here. I will send you more information shortly as I receive it," Nathaniel said.

"Of course," Aria squeaked.

Luannie exchanged several glances with Sebastian, as neither one knew how to digest the news or console Aria as she wept into her arms over the steering wheel. Luannie thought about Nathaniel's appearance this morning and recalled how equally tousled he was as Aria is now. They both appeared physically and emotionally drained.

Aria apologized for her sorrow and promised to show them around the Linnaeus Garden another time and talk about the situation later once she knew more. Luannie and Sebastian didn't bother fastening their seat belts on the way back to their rooms, but they did lean on one another as they wept during the ride, with light music playing in the background.

The elevator rang as it reached the fourth floor, and Luannie scraped their feet through the hallway.

"Hold up," Sebastian said, his movements slowing to a complete stop.

Luannie felt dreary, and a heavy feeling of exhaustion lured them to bed.

Sebastian was looking straight through Luannie's head, and he seemed to want to make the muscles in his legs and arms move forward, but he stood still on the elevator platform.

"You good?" Luannie stepped toward him. "You look a little funny."

The muscles in Sebastian's face tightened as he fought against some resistance to exit the elevator. His fingers were fidgeting, and he released a grunt when he tried to speak. He tried to break through whatever force was keeping him still, but then he shifted his eyes onto

Luannie and concentrated on the idea of calmly joining them in the hallway.

Suddenly, Sebastian's legs catapulted him forward. When he made his way beside Luannie, another force hit him, stopping him in his tracks. *Ugh!* He bent over and rested an elbow on Luannie's shoulder, nearly falling over, although able to move normally again.

"You know what?" He let the unfinished thought linger before kissing the crystal around his neck. "Let's figure this out."

Samara's room was nearest to the elevator, just across from the medical room. "You think we should knock? See if she's awake?" Luannie suggested. "She probably doesn't know yet."

"Uh," Sebastian stammered, eyeing his room at the other end of the hall. He gave in. "I guess."

Knock knock. Knock knock. The rhythm reminded Luannie of a heartbeat, and they instantly thought of Jaewon.

Knock knock. Knock knock.

Samara opened the door with her Shayla wrapped as neatly as she could get it within a few knocks. Strands of shiny black hair hung and framed her face. "Morning," she said through a yawn, and she didn't follow up with anything else.

"Sorry to wake you," Luannie said.

"Oh, no, I've been awake for a while. Just haven't felt like doing much of anything." Samara was talking to the walls of her room as she panned around, looking at everything besides Luannie and Sebastian.

"Have you heard?" Sebastian asked.

Samara scratched at her face and stared at the floor. "Yeah, I was the last to know. I still can't believe it. We only just met, and now he's no longer with us. It's like…"

Luannie's mind wandered on how they enjoyed hanging out with Jaewon, talking with him, eating with him, falling asleep on his bedroom floor. They wondered if he was still wearing the necklace they'd given him a few days ago when Samara disrupted their memory.

"I wish I'd stayed longer in his room with you all last night. If only he had stayed in the medical room, our program directors could've checked in on him."

Sebastian brushed both of his palms over his head and expelled a shot of breath. "It's just not right. Aria said she'd be speaking with us all later."

Samara frowned, and the realization hit Luannie that they'd barely gotten to know Jaewon and yet felt as though they had just lost a childhood companion.

"Millie mentioned speaking to his mom on the phone before calling me. I can't imagine what that woman must be going through," Samara said. "Sending her son to start school in another country and then receiving news like this, never able to see him again? She must be devastated." Samara tilted her head back.

Sebastian tugged on the back of Luannie's shirt, making them jump.

"Well, I'm going to head to my room and lay down for a while. I need to rest," Luannie said, and they could sense Sebastian nodding his head behind them.

"I'll see you two later." Samara pushed her chin out toward them. "Let's all get some rest for now."

Luannie headed down the hall past Jaewon's room, glancing at the door. When they stopped in front of theirs, Sebastian pressed his hand flat against it to keep it from opening.

"Looks like I was onto something earlier."

"What?" Luannie asked with a slight smirk.

"Millie is a program director, teacher, medical assistant, and also apparently a woman of many languages." He borrowed the smirk Luannie had made, and they exchanged theirs for a flat line. "Because Jaewon's mom only speaks Korean."

CHAPTER XIII

Samara showered and allowed her mind to race through the events of the past few days. She lathered, massaged, and rinsed her hair for half an hour as the bathroom turned into a steam room and opened her pores. The showerhead scattered drops of period blood to either side of the shower floor, and Samara bathed her mid-drift, taking a moment to feel the indentations of her light stretch marks. Despite being of a thin stature, she found herself brushing fingers over cellulite that appeared all around her body. Samara stretched tall and reached backward until there was a satisfying cracking of her vertebrae, which only briefly brought a contented smile to her face.

It was late morning when Samara heard a knocking at her front door where she was dressed in blue tones and flossing her naturally straight teeth. *I don't want to stay here. I want to go back home, or at least back to when Jaewon was still with us.*

"Hello," Aria greeted Samara as she opened the door. "Just a reminder that we'll be gathering in the meeting room down the hall directly across from Sebastian's in fifteen minutes."

Samara mouthed "okay" and bowed into her room to retreat into herself. Aria had called for a group meeting earlier with the scholars to have "healthy conversations about well-being, have time for grieving," and "address schedule updates due to recent circumstances."

Samara understood why the language was vague and sugary, but part of her wanted to say, "No, be direct. Jaewon died this morning, and now you want to make sure none of us are getting any ideas." She finished assembling herself and made her way down the hall. The multi-purpose room was across Jaewon's, and across from Luannie's was a door labeled "Storage." The meeting room across from Sebastian's was the last place Samara felt like entering at this time.

"Thanks for joining us," Aria said as Samara entered last.

Four chairs sat positioned in a circle, with three being a bit closer than the outlier where Aria sat. Samara flattened her lips in an uneasy smile and sat to the right of Luannie. The emptiness between her and Luannie was physically small, and yet she felt this space was supposed to be held by where Jaewon would usually be and should have been seated. Samara didn't look over, but she sensed that both Luannie and Sebastian were downcast, though not nearly as much as she.

"Before we get into everything, I'd like for us all to try a couple of minutes of relaxing meditation. It will help get us into a calmer state." After that, Aria didn't provide further instruction, so Samara waited for a few seconds and then tried mimicking what Sebastian had done. Sebastian's feet were shoulder-width apart on the floor, the backs of his hands on his thighs, his back against the support of the chair, and his chest slowly rising and falling. Samara couldn't help but peek every few seconds to see if anyone else had their eyes open. She felt juvenile attempting to be mindful in front of these people as she stared at her inner eyelids. Although meditation wasn't necessarily religious, it felt spiritual. She dedicated herself to the meditation, thinking about how Sebastian was so well grounded in his own spiritual life and wanting that kind of strength for herself at the moment.

"Okay." Aria released a long breath. "Now, I spent a large portion of the day speaking with Millie and Nathaniel. We've brainstormed a few ideas about what we can do next, but first, we want to see what's most appealing to you. We came up with options for tomorrow: take a day for personal rest, go as a group on a simple trip somewhere nearby, or spend the day doing activities together at the campus. How do you all think these options sound?"

Samara forced her eyes from rolling back. Aria's suggestions reminded Samara of a time in her youth when her mother needed to stay home to watch her because her father had an important event and nobody else was available to chaperone. Not that a mature Samara at the age of only nine years felt she needed one. "Here is what you can do," her mother proposed in Arabic. "You can spend the day playing in your room, watching television, praying, or whatever else you feel like doing that isn't going to be disruptive. Do you understand?"

Samara didn't care what she and the other two scholars decided to do tomorrow for the most part, so long as she found time for herself along the way.

"I don't know," Sebastian said. "I don't want to be alone, but the campus isn't somewhere I want to be right now, and going for a trip feels wrong without Jaewon."

"Yeah, maybe we could all find something to do someplace else without making a big deal of it," Luannie added.

Aria's eyes fell on Samara now.

"Sure, that makes sense," Samara offered, pressured to give her piece. *More?* "I don't want to do too much, either. Anything is fine with me."

"All right," Aria confirmed. "Then I will speak with Millie and Nathaniel again later today and get back to you all tonight on something we can do as a group tomorrow— that isn't an excursion."

Then, Aria paused to scroll through something on her phone silently and began to read from the screen. "We understand that being in Sweden is a new experience for all of you. Not much time has passed to begin your immersion into the culture, but enough time *has* passed to form meaningful bonds with one another. Should you wish to reconsider your stay in this program, we respect your concerns and are happy to discuss further options with you. Be assured, the School of International Relations' faculty and staff is honored to have you here as our first cohort of International Scholars. Your safety is our top priority, and we would like to ensure each of you is physically and mentally safe during your stay here." Aria lowered her neck along with her voice. "To honor the recent loss of our fellow friend and scholar, Jaewon, let's take a moment of silence to reflect on his passing and how grateful we all are to have gotten to know him over these past few days…"

Samara felt the silence, heard the silence, and saw the silence on Luannie and Sebastian's somber expressions. It was a sudden pause in the room that felt like a drawn-out end. She swiftly opened the Uppsala Map app on her phone and typed a location in the search bar. The quickest arrival time to the place was fifty-two minutes by car.

"Should any of you want to talk about your well-being or anything else at all, please feel free to reach out," Aria continued. "We are committed to being here for you for the duration of your academic year here in Sweden and are truly thrilled to have you with us. We will get through this. As always, if anyone would like to speak further, please get in touch with me. I welcome you all to talk with me sometime today or this week, and I will do my best to make you feel comfortable."

Did she write this? Why was it so long, so official? Is she going to be speaking with us one and one at some point? Samara picked at her skin, taking pinch after pinch of her left forearm between her right thumb and index finger as she gradually became consumed with anxiety, uncertainty, and some other feeling she couldn't identify.

After the meeting, the scholars shuffled into the hall behind Aria, who wished them a good day. Sebastian invited Samara to join him and Luannie in his room for a while, but without hesitation, she politely declined. Samara headed down the hall and into her room. She spent less than a minute inside until throwing the door back open with her face buried into her phone and headed toward the elevator.

My father will be understanding if I leave, but my mother wants me to stick to this program more than anything. She'll be so disappointed if I give up.

Samara walked down the street and entered a small taxi-pod that had recently pulled up to the curb.

"Samara?" the driver asked, mispronouncing her name.

"Mhmm," she replied while intently watching the pointer on her phone map until it began to move with the car.

The ride was no more than an hour, but it felt to Samara as though she had been watching the streets of Sweden zoom past her for no more than three minutes. The taxi confirmed the upcoming destination and pulled over in front of a silver and white twelve-story building. She passed Swedish Armed Forces guards, swiped her hand over the entrance keypad, and entered the lobby. Dozens of microchip providers sat at tables and invited people up from their turn in line. Samara walked past the snaked line of one hundred or so people and unlocked the elevator in the back of the lobby. Her microchip was programmed to access the entrance, the tenth floor, and one other floor.

"*Labb, nivå två*, lab level two," a monotone voice announced as the elevator door opened on the second-lowest laboratory floor at Chipd.

The elevator door slid open, and Samara saw a tall figure holding a long instrument that held onto a tiny object. Nova lingered it over a box on the table in front of her, and when the elevator door dinged shut, she dropped it inside and removed her gloves, then her specs.

Samara walked further into the laboratory and through several rows of microchip samples, all containing alternate variations of their capabilities. The space Nova was laboring in was behind an electronic shield that protected her ongoing work from being manipulated, as it was impenetrable against external signals of any kind. Samara stood on the other side where she knew the field existed and watched as it crackled and powered off.

"Come in," Nova invited her without peering up.

Samara was in awe at the gadgets that filled this small room. There must have been thousands of tested microchips that weren't yet up to Nova's par, and she could sense Nova's smile.

"I figured you might come. Have you been getting along with the scholars?" Nova asked.

"Nova," Samara stated boldly and moved closer to her. "What the hell have you done?"

Nova wiggled her fingers and looked upon the pieces on her work table. "You don't have to curse."

Samara fiercely tore the instrument from Nova's hand and threw it into the electric shield that enclosed them both, making it glitch. "Am I the only one using my head here? Jaewon just started questioning me in front of the other two last night, and then he commits suicide? No one's reading that story."

Nova rolled her eyes, picked up another instrument on the table, and faced Samara. "I'm not cruel. I let him see a place he's wanted to visit with his mother as he fell. Something you informed me of, by the way."

Samara grimaced, recalling how much Jaewon wanted to visit Pyeongchang County.

"For someone who claims to be using her head, you're far into yours. Remember all of this?" Nova over-articulated as she waved her fingers in circles. "*This* is the plan. Jaewon has played his part," she continued in a high-pitched, condescending tone and tapped on two used microchips that lay in a box on the table. "It's a bit damaged because the boy decided to land on his head. But we still have the chips in the others. I am wondering, though, do you think any program director will look into this further than necessary?"

Samara glared at Jaewon's brain microchip on the table, and it was next to another one that Nova inserted into his hand at the campus.

"Well, we certainly don't need to worry about Mattias anymore." Nova swiped a few times on her phone and showed Samara her screen. It was a television segment reporting on the death of Chipd employee Mattias Rozelle. "He went public with the idea he gave me before I could."

Samara peered at what else was on the project tables. "More prototypes? We're not even done conducting tests and gathering information from the ones already placed!" She poked her head a few times. "They are aware that something isn't right with their heads."

Nova grew a Cheshire cat smile and put her specs back on her face. They hovered over her nose and buzzed as they extended toward the piece she was analyzing while the other side of the specs moved closer toward her eye. "Shouldn't you be spending quality time with the subjects? You can't be getting to know them while you're standing here with me."

CHAPTER XIV

Sebastian divided three strands of hair on one side of Luannie's head and began swinging them through one another. It had been about an hour since he left the meeting room, nearly lunchtime now, and Luannie had agreed to let him create a six-strand braid in their hair. Sebastian's fingers were smooth as the silky waves continuously ran through. Sebastian's mother had taught him how to do this at a young age, along with other skills. She taught him how to sew, braid, tie different knots, cook family dishes, fix appliances, construct furniture, and budget. After weaving the two sets of braids in Luannie's hair together, he laid it at the side of their left shoulder.

"Thank you. I love it," Luannie said, adoring the braid.

Sebastian's suspicions revolving around Nathaniel floated back to the surface of his mind. "Do you think Nathaniel was just parked outside campus this morning waiting to go inside?"

Luannie shrugged. "Maybe he felt the same sense of danger that I had."

Sebastian studied Luannie's face as it bent, questioning the suggestion. "What's got me bothered still is how Millie insisted on getting Jaewon out of the hospital. Why not take a few more X-rays?"

"Yeah, I've thought about that too. And what about Millie saying she spoke with Jaewon's mom?" Luannie lingered an open left palm over their new braid, feeling over the twists a few times, and then they touched the part of their hand where their microchip lay underneath.

"I wonder if we should let Aria know that Samara chose to be alone after the meeting. Is it any of our business? No," Sebastian answered himself. "But it's cruel to leave her alone if her worries are starting to consume her. Who knows what she's feeling? I've been feeling off ever since we arrived here. I mean, I remember the first time entering this room and feeling so exhausted. That feeling hasn't changed much."

Luannie leaned forward off the bed and then steadily stood into a stretch that reminded Sebastian of the shape of a sprouting leaf reaching for sunlight.

"What was going on when you were on the elevator earlier?" Luannie asked before turning around to face Sebastian. "I wanted to help, but I wasn't sure how."

"Ahh," Sebastian sighed and got onto his feet. "I can't make sense of something that doesn't make sense. It'll lose me. I'm not sure who the voice I heard belongs to, but somebody told me to try and move forward. When I tried to walk toward you, I couldn't. The voice said I couldn't move until I focused less on the command or action and more on the end goal. They spoke almost as if giving me a riddle," he whispered as if it were a secret. "I was only able to move again when I stopped thinking about it, and I simply stared ahead and let my mind go blank."

They stood side by side, facing in opposite directions. "Considering it isn't a symptom of shock from the trauma we've been through," they teased, echoing Sebastian's words earlier that morning, "what do you want to do about it?"

They looked at one another and around the room, a bit helpless. Sebastian refused to allow the uncertainty of the week's events to get the best of him or Luannie, and he didn't want either of them going down a similar path as Jaewon.

Four consecutive knocks.

"Samara?" Sebastian guessed.

Luannie opened the door a crack and jumped back with a loud gasp. They opened the door wider and stared. Aria stood as close as she could have stood without entering the room, and Sebastian noticed the twitching in her upper left arm.

"Is she in here?" Aria asked quickly with her neck twisting to take a look around Sebastian's room.

"Samara?" Luannie clarified, still catching their breath.

"She's not?" Aria paused and locked her eyes on the hair supplies that sat at Sebastian's feet. Then she looked up to him. "Are you sure?"

Sebastian grabbed his School of International Relations tote bag and slipped on his shoes while Luannie watched and followed suit as Aria rambled on in his bedroom doorway.

"Well, she must not be here then. I mean, she isn't in her room. Where could she have gone? An hour is a long time to be missing without any contact. It's my job as a program director to look after all of you, and yet I'm standing here asking you things that I should already know the answers to!" Aria abruptly stopped her spew. She recognized that Luannie and Sebastian were standing in front of her, ready to accompany her searching for Samara.

A small smile grew on Aria's face into the smile Sebastian remembered her having the day he sat by her in that café in Stockholm. He and Luannie followed her out of the building, and he thought back on the conversation he'd had with Aria that day. She had advised that Sebastian would grow accustomed to it here and make friends with the other scholars while away from everyone and everything familiar. Assessing himself now, he could say most of those things were true.

"I asked Nathaniel to see if the Public Health Agency could share Samara's location with us, but he said he was away tonight." Aria scoffed and fluttered her eyelids. "Away." She tapped her hand to the car door, and for the second time today, Luannie and Sebastian got into the backseat.

"We invited Samara to spend time with us, but she said she'd rather go to her room. Maybe she's more upset about Jaewon than she's letting on," Luannie proposed.

"Well, even if that's the case, I need to know where she is. She could get lost or do something unsafe." Aria bit her lip and slammed on the gas, sending both Luannie and Sebastian backward in their seats.

"I bet everything's all right," Sebastian said as he saw the café pass from outside the car window. "Maybe she went for a walk," he added with hope. *I hadn't yet considered what Aria might know.*

Aria screeched to a stop outside of the campus building. Sebastian didn't have much time to think before getting out of the car because Aria was already out and entering the front door. The lights turned on as Aria entered the main room, and Sebastian watched her turn around, thinking of which room to look in first. Aria decided to search the technology room.

"I guess I can check out the second floor. I haven't gotten the chance to see it, anyway," Luannie said as they entered the campus building with Sebastian.

Sebastian didn't want to have a déjà vu of the last time he used the elevator. "Okay, let me know if you need anything." He patted where his phone sat in his pants pocket.

Luannie scanned their chip, pressed a few buttons, and got onto the elevator. As soon as it closed, Sebastian glanced around the lobby by himself.

His reflection on the television startled him. Then his eyes wandered just left of the television to where he remembered Nathaniel mentioning there was a door the scholars wouldn't have to use. He couldn't tell where the door's outline was because it blended in seamlessly with the wall. Sebastian brushed his hand over to see if he could feel anything and then waved his left hand, hoping he'd hover it over where the microchip scans.

After a few aimless swipes, there was a click. The door unlocked and rolled upward into the wall. A winding staircase seemed to lead above to the second floor. Sebastian took another look around the lobby. He looked to the windows, half expecting and half wanting Nathaniel to be running in from across the street. Sebastian felt for a light switch near the staircase but could only see that the steps twisted 180 degrees. *Why the hell would someone design steps like this?*

Luannie used the buttons to send the elevator horizontally along the second floor. They saw empty, unused rooms they suspected were what the program directors referred to as "classrooms." There were no lockers or vending machines in sight, and nothing stood out besides the enclosed hall that connected two walls. It cut across the main room and was located just above the lobby on the first floor.

A loud crackling sound startled Sebastian. He didn't see anyone behind him in the lobby, but the sound of static instilled a fear in him that he couldn't rationalize. Sebastian glanced around the stairs as far as he could, and when he realized he wouldn't be able to make anything out without eventually climbing them, he backed out of the door and into the main room.

To Sebastian's right, lights from the television flickered with changing screens that were playing on the news. He watched as the volume went up from twenty-three, twenty-five, twenty-seven, twenty-nine, thirty-one. A news segment was playing that showed lines of people waiting to get their microchips placed by employees inside Chipd Headquarters. A couple of dozen tables were on the main floor, and Sebastian watched as the reporter spoke about the night's success while zooming in on people's hands.

Sebastian touched the area under his skin where his microchip sat, and it reminded him of the day the scholars got theirs. He thought of how Jaewon strutted up to Millie as she was speaking and practically demanded she give him those release forms without saying a word, his arm outstretched and his face expressionless. Sebastian was grateful that Luannie and himself were still considerably consistent in their behavioral patterns.

Sebastian turned to his right to look at where the technology room was behind him but stopped midway at the sight of someone peeping in from the other side of the front door. He heard his gasp followed by another from the open elevator behind him. Luannie got off the elevator platform and joined Sebastian in the lobby as Millie unlocked the front door.

She approached the two of them with her eyes squinted and lips parted. "I didn't expect to see you two here."

Luannie and Sebastian remained silent.

"Hmm. Should I be concerned? Have you two eaten lunch yet?" Millie examined the scholars' faces.

Sebastian was aware that he looked as skeptical as he was. "We didn't get the chance to see the second floor yesterday, so we thought we'd stop by," he lied, not trusting Millie, and he was proud of how quickly he answered.

"Oh, Aria told Nathaniel and me that visiting campus would be too distressing at this time. You two are here without Samara?" Millie asked.

"Aria told us she needed help finding her, and she isn't responding to her phone," Sebastian shared.

Millie looked at Sebastian as he took several glances at the television before looking at it herself. "Sebastian, is something wrong?"

Sebastian now saw several lab technicians surrounding a human brain model on the screen, pointing at it in sections separated by a marker with an "X" located near the top, making Sebastian feel queasy. He no longer heard the television; a muted emoticon turned on in the lower left-hand corner of the screen, and he could only hear a loud buzzing in his ears.

"Sebastian?" Luannie asked.

He turned to them, ignoring Millie's original inquiry. "What are they doing?" he asked Luannie, pointing to the screen on the wall.

"On the television?" they asked.

"What they're talking about, doesn't that—"

"Who's talking?" Millie asked him. "Are you watching something on here?"

"Yes, but it's muted now," he responded.

"It's not even on," Luannie whispered.

Sebastian continued watching as the brain got poked and prodded, simultaneously feeling sharp pains around his own. He wanted to believe Luannie because he trusted them, but the fact that neither they nor Millie could see what was on the television screen disturbed him.

Millie looked toward the technology room from where Aria had just emerged. She didn't wait for Aria to finish greeting and ask her for help. Millie walked toward Aria and then passed her without stopping. "Can you join me in here for a moment?"

Aria watched Millie enter the technology room. "Okay, we're going to talk, and I'll be right back," Aria told the scholars, evidently flustered. "Are you two all right? I guess Samara's not here, huh?"

Sebastian wasn't sure if he could tell Aria, Luannie, or Millie whether he was indeed all right.

"Yeah, we're fine," Luannie answered for the two of them.

"We shouldn't be very long. Please be careful," Aria said with a sweet smile, and the scholars gladly returned it.

Sebastian waited for the door to the technology room to close and then opened the door near the television that closed while he watched the lights flickering on the TV before Millie arrived.

"Luannie, you really couldn't see anything playing on the television?" he asked.

"Nothing," they told him, looking at him sideways.

He shook his head up and down and proceeded to creep up the steps.

"So, what do you think is up here? Do you think Samara is here?" Luannie asked.

"Nope," Sebastian answered. "I don't think she's here at all. While you checked upstairs, I remembered Nathaniel told us that we would never need to go in this room. But what if he meant we were never *supposed* to go in here?" He neared the top of the staircase and couldn't make out anything in front of him. It looked as though the stairs led to a wall or another door. "Did you see anything upstairs?"

"The lights turned on as I walked down the hall, and I didn't see much," Luannie responded. "The rooms don't look like classrooms or offices, and it looks abandoned as if the first floor of this place is the only one in use." They waited for Sebastian to move further up the steps. "Well?"

"Another door maybe," Sebastian said. He knew it made no sense for a door to lead to another door. If anything, perhaps the design of the staircase was to serve its purpose as a deterrent. Nonetheless, he waved his left hand in the air and hoped to hear the click of a door unlocking.

The sound of a door opening gave him hope, but he realized it was coming from downstairs in the lobby. Sebastian and Luannie looked at one another, and Luannie put their index finger in front of their mouth. The door to the technology room closed, and the sound of footsteps walked toward the front door of the campus building.

Sebastian motioned a story with his hands, but Luannie held back a giggle because his movements weren't precise. Sebastian stuck out a finger to remind them not to make noise. He pointed a finger around the stairs and motioned his hand down to ask if the door had closed, and Luannie checked and nodded yes. The two of them peered at the twist in the staircase as the person in the lobby walked nearby. The sounds of footsteps stopped near the television and then picked up again, going toward the elevator. Sebastian released a breath without realizing he was holding it and heard the elevator door ring and close.

Luannie mouthed, "Should we go?" to Sebastian while nodding down the staircase. He shook his head side to side, waving his hand aimlessly around the wall. There was a click, but a door didn't slide up. The click came from the other side of the door, and he realized somebody else had entered through the other side of the room that Sebastian and Luannie were trying to enter.

"Let's go, now. I remember seeing an enclosed hall on the second floor. That must be what this door leads to," Luannie whispered with enunciation to Sebastian.

With a look of disappointment, he agreed and followed them back down the stairs. Noises came from the room at the top of the staircase. Sebastian noticed the television wasn't on in the lobby anymore, and Luannie walked briskly for the front door.

"Wait," Sebastian hissed.

Luannie turned around with wide eyes and upward palms.

He could feel them watching as he approached the door to the technology room and waved his hand over it, but it wasn't unlocking. He looked back at Luannie and back to the door. Luannie started walking over to try using their microchip, too, but they heard someone get onto the elevator platform from the floor above them.

Sebastian and Luannie made a run for the front door and turned down the street in the opposite direction from the housing building.

"Her car is still here," Sebastian said as he ran, pointing toward Aria's car.

"I don't know what Millie's car looks like, but someone's in there snooping around that hall," Luannie answered as clearly as they could while running.

Neither saw, but somebody stood in front of campus and watched as they ran around the corner.

CHAPTER XV

Sebastian and Luannie ran neck and neck down the opposite side of the block from the campus building. There weren't many other people outside, but flocks of birds flew overhead across from the lamp posts.

Sebastian began to wind down and watched as Luannie turned their neck and slowed their pace in front of him.

"What?" Luannie asked, coming to a stop.

Sebastian looked behind him, back to Luannie, then down at the shadow he cast on the sidewalk and softly laughed at it.

"What the hell?" Luannie pushed through with airy breath.

Sebastian shrugged his shoulders. "What are we doing right now?" He threw his arms out to his sides and spun around in a circle. "Who are we even running from?" His head was tilted backward, facing up at the sky.

Luannie blew out exhaust from their mouth, both amused and annoyed by his behavior.

Sebastian started gesturing as he continued listing his questions, "Is anyone chasing us? Where are we going?"

Luannie searched Sebastian's eyes for tranquility, and he dropped his arms to his sides, along with the muscles in his face. "We both felt unsafe back there, right?"

"Sure," Sebastian responded, "but do we think Millie is chasing us right now? If she wanted to, she could get in her car and drive after us. Or better yet," Sebastian was now motioning his arms in such a dramatic way that he reminded himself of Nathaniel, "she could just ask the Public Health Agency to pinpoint our location!"

There was stillness in the air as the birds remained on their lamp posts. Sebastian grew aware of how riled up he had become. Acting this way unsettled him because separating himself from the inexplicable experiences he had recently was something he prided himself on. Sebastian didn't want the experiences to combine with reality. He adjusted his stance and let out a laugh, uncomfortable with how his irritability made him feel weak.

"You know, I know when to pick my battles, and I have no desire to stick around to deal with any of this," he said as he motioned his pointer fingers upward to the building rooftops, "just to end up like Jaewon."

Luannie's concerned look turned into a frown after his last few words. Sebastian stared at his feet. He knew he didn't mean any disrespect by it, and Sebastian knew that

Luannie knew that too, but he still felt obliged to spend a moment in reflection.

It began to drizzle, and Luannie pulled out their phone.

Sebastian peeped over. "What are you looking at?" he asked, but they didn't reply. Sebastian noticed how unruly Luannie's hair looked, frizz sticking out of the braids. He shifted onto his other leg and looked back toward the street corner, unsure of what or who he was checking. "Luannie?" Sebastian tried asking again. Then he heard his phone *ding*, and he removed it from his pants pocket and read Luannie's message on the School of IR app.

Did you get this? Message me back, it said. He responded, swiping away drops of rain, and heard the alert for his new message sound from Luannie's phone shortly after.

Luannie slanted their head as they read his message. *Have you tried reaching out to your family at all? Any contact?* he had written.

Sebastian dragged himself over to the nearest building wall and leaned against it. The truth is, he had tried reaching out to his parents several times since he activated his phone but never heard back.

"I know we don't have our phone numbers set up yet, but none of my messages or calls, even through social media, have gotten a response since we got these phone SIM cards." Sebastian listened to the flapping of the bird's wings as they resumed flight between lamp posts. The image of dampened feathers flapping under rainfall compelled him to stretch out his arms. He looked over at Luannie, who now accompanied him against the wall.

"Me neither. I would've expected at least one of my parents to check in on me. But not even my brother responded…" They lowered their head and added, "I don't think they're getting our messages."

Sebastian knew that Luannie was probably right. Knowing that Luannie also hadn't heard back from their family provided him with only a momentary comfort. He had never felt so trapped, so distanced from others and himself as he had since arriving in Sweden. He no longer bothered thinking up logical explanations for what he and the other scholars had been experiencing. Instead, it was the interpersonal relations over the past week which disturbed him most.

I can't lose contact with Luannie.

"Should we report something to someone?" Sebastian asked.

Luannie answered with the thought that immediately followed in Sebastian's head.

"Report what, exactly, to who? People will think we're playing around, or worse, being serious." Luannie picked at their short fingernails, painted burgundy, and clasped their hands together. The rain was pulling down the frizziness that had surrounded Luannie's braids, making it difficult to see the excellent job Sebastian had done at making them. "Do you want to go home? Your real home?" they asked in a higher octave than they typically spoke with while keeping their eyes glued to the sidewalk.

Sebastian stared at the side of Luannie's face, its outline long and ovular. Their eyebrows were prominent, eyelashes naturally curled, and a bead of sweat or rain on their nose hovered just above their full lips, at which they were gnawing.

For every reason Sebastian could think of to answer Luannie's question, the answer was yes, except one. He could always attend another school or visit Sweden at another time. He wanted to remove himself from the School of International Relations and reconnect with his family, which would also mean returning to Brazil while Luannie returned to Hawaii. The idea of not spending any more time together was daunting despite his stubborn independence. *But what good is being near a friend when it may very well be keeping us both in danger?*

The drizzle from the clouds turned into light rain, and thin bolts of lightning accompanied an increasingly graying sky. They were white, skinny, and reminded Sebastian of veins from the tree of knowledge, also referred to as the tree of life. He interpreted the tree as a metaphor for being punished when using reason and free-thinking, and he wondered again about Samara's whereabouts.

Suddenly, Sebastian felt struck along the core of his spine, and he abruptly snapped backward. An intense rush passed through his body, crackling, making him jump forward. He saw Luannie out of the corner of his eyes. His heart was racing, and the feeling of electric volts surging throughout his veins distracted him from the swirl of birds surrounding the nearest lamp post. He clenched his jaw and tried not to look pained in front of Luannie, who was now standing open-mouthed as he wriggled in discomfort. He could only see lightning in the distance, and no bolts were long enough to reach the ground, yet he felt as though he was electrocuted.

Sebastian felt a sense of release, as though a stranglehold had let go. He panted heavily. "Let's just… f-focus on getting someplace right now."

Luannie took a cautious step closer to him, but he would not meet their gaze. "Okay," they whispered uncertainly. "Where are we going?" When Sebastian didn't respond, Luannie suggested, "Let's just have a seat." They motioned for Sebastian to sit down with them on the curb in a parental manner, patting the air.

Sebastian closed his eyes and wiggled his head. A shock of electricity shook him and raced up and down his spine. His shoulders lifted, and his head shrunk into his neck.

"Ugh!" He groaned. He shook his arms in front of him and released a final "No!" His eyes snapped open, and he started running like a bat out of hell down the street. The lightning-quick movement scared the birds that weren't already swirling around into a frenzy.

"Sebastian!" he heard Luannie call after him.

The air was still, but Sebastian cut through it swiftly and generated a wind that whipped past his face. His toes barely touched the ground as he sprinted down the sidewalk. Sebastian couldn't stop running with his leg muscles energized, and his mind focused on nothing more than the action of propelling himself forward. He felt fully charged.

After what seemed to him to be a few seconds later, Sebastian became aware of his surroundings. Not once did he make a turn while running, and yet, he passed Luannie where they had both been standing together moments before, and Luannie was still in the middle of calling his name after him. Sebastian couldn't turn around but could dart his eyes side to side. He noticed again: he passed Luannie in the same place from where he had begun running. His lungs were burning, his nose stinging, and his legs aching as Sebastian continued running in circles around the block. His mind finally registered that, no matter how far he seemed to run, he kept looping and flashing past Luannie at the same point in time without the self-control to stop himself.

After what felt like two miles within two minutes, the wind rushing past Sebastian stopped, as did his feet mid-sprint, and his body jolted forward while his shoes remained planted on the ground. Sebastian felt the pain in his face from where he fell on the sidewalk, having had very little time to extend his arms out in front of him.

The wind that his energy generated was no longer cooling him, and the air was still now, muggy and stiff. He stared at the concrete beneath him, and his lips trembled. Drops of blood fell from his nose and created a wet stain above the sidewalk crack, the size of a quarter. There weren't many times in Sebastian's life where he couldn't control his actions or make sense of what was happening to him, and this new sense of dissociation made his eyes swell with tears.

To Sebastian's left was the café that Jaewon supposedly tripped in front of, but Sebastian was sure he did not trip there just now, either. The plant sat on the ground at eye level and taunted him. Sebastian used his hands to raise his torso and hovered as he bent his neck to look up in front of him, noticing his stomach rumble from having missed both breakfast and lunch.

Millie was standing in front of the campus building, peering down at the other end of the street. She pulled out her phone to message somebody and waited for a *ding* in response, then started walking to her car. She didn't seem to notice Sebastian there, but he watched as she got into her vehicle and pulled onto the street.

Luannie, he thought from the opposite side of the street. Millie's car began driving down the road, and a pair of eyes met Sebastian's through the rearview mirror.

CHAPTER XVI

A mug of espresso sat on the dining table at Herman's Restaurant in the mid-afternoon. Hot steam rose and blended into the air, adding to the heat that spilled into the dining area from the kitchen. Nathaniel's fingers grasped the handle and drew the mug in close enough to stir with a reusable coffee stick. Herman's was empty except for non-patrons who entered to use the restroom and a group of middle-aged adults who gathered at the bar to reminisce on their pasts together. He swirled the espresso with the stick a few times before lifting the mug to his mouth. Nathaniel stopped just short of taking a sip and looked at the front door, half of his face covered by the cup and his green eyes covered by steam.

She pulled the door wide open in one sweeping motion, drawing attention from a couple of drinkers at the bar, and strutted over to where Nathaniel sat alone in the middle of the restaurant. One side of the collar of her blazer was standing up and framing her expressionless face. A top knot that usually gathered neatly on the crown of her head was coming undone, a few wisps of whitish-blond hair falling over her pale blue eyes. Millie stood in front of the table, watching as Nathaniel resumed his sip of espresso before she took a seat across from him.

Nathaniel noticed his appearance in the mug's reflection as he placed it down. His dark hair, the resulting features from his Swedish and Italian background, was unintentionally messy, and his eyebrow hairs stood in more than one direction. The pressure of Millie's stare weighed down on him, and Nathaniel traced his eyes around her as if there were a circle of space before him into which Nathaniel could not look directly. He let air escape his mouth and pressed his fists into his cheeks, sliding his elbows forward on the table.

"Don't lean," Millie advised him.

Nathaniel chuckled with barely any movement in his face and readjusted his posture. He could tell his eyes looked glossy because he felt wetness transfer between his lower and upper eyelashes as he blinked, thinking about how Jaewon had appeared carried out of the ambulance and into the hospital. The blood...

"I started working at Chipd to be part of a team that creates breakthrough technology to *help* people, not destroy them. I did *not* agree to any of this," Nathaniel stated firmly, his hands clenching in and out of fists.

"Why so sad?" Millie asked in a tone that was neither caring nor condescending, yet both—a skill that takes practice to master. She didn't see his eyes glare into hers after that remark because a waiter approached to take her order. Nathaniel watched as Millie dismissed the man, reassured him of the dismissal, and then requested three shots of espresso.

Millie looked over to Nathaniel, but he was now observing the stick swirling in his mug.

"Honestly, you can't be this distraught," she said with a wince. Millie reached into her purse and extended her hand for Nathaniel to take her phone. After a second of waiting, she firmly placed it on the table and pushed the phone toward him. "They're asking for two replacements."

Nathaniel widened his wet eyes, which sat on top of two swollen cheeks. He didn't bother to swipe at the tears that fell onto them when he blinked. He was enticed by the swirling motion the stick made in his mug of barely drunken espresso.

"Well…" She looked up and counted with her lips. "We need four, actually," Millie updated him.

Nathaniel whipped his face up and grimaced at Millie's slanted lips. *Four?* he questioned to himself incredulously. *Who other than Mattias and Jaewon?* Nathaniel moved his arms aimlessly underneath the table. Just as he opened his mouth to speak, Nathaniel was caught off guard by Millie's hand slamming down onto the phone, which sat in front of him, and she slid it back toward herself.

Nathaniel rose from his seat abruptly, sending the chair back and again drawing attention from the group at the bar. One was so drunk, he was dipping his finger into a martini.

"I will *not* continue this way," Nathaniel insisted loudly. He left his drink and glided with his long legs out of Herman's toward his car. His hands twitched as he slipped the ring from his left finger off and into his pocket.

A swipe of Nathaniel's hand across the dashboard turned on the radio, interrupted by a phone alert that sounded through the speakers. He read the sender's name with relief and locked eyes on the notification, tapped it open, and sped away from the curb before he could fully finish reading the message.

A car screeched to a park in front of where Sebastian sat on the sidewalk. The underside of his shoes touched one another, and his palms faced upward on his knees. Sebastian heard the car approach, followed by a door slamming, but he remained seated with his eyes closed. He was trying to steady his breath and maintain as much mental clarity as possible with each held inhale and slow exhale. There was still some blood beneath his nostril leftover from his bloody nose after slamming into the sidewalk. But a strong scent of cologne permeated the air around him and inspired Sebastian to open his eyes.

Sebastian first saw the scuffed, pointed black business shoes that Nathaniel wore, just above which were a pair of royal blue colored straight pants that appeared silky and snug. A jet black button-down was no longer tucked with the bottom-most button undone and the shirt's collar loosened. Nathaniel had his blazer draped over his left shoulder, supported by his left pointer finger as his right hand formed a fist that rested on his right hip. Then Sebastian saw the unruly hair, and he took a moment to digest this image. Without speaking, he stood up slowly and led Nathaniel into the lobby of the housing building.

Sebastian noticed Nathaniel nod to the front desk attendant, who quickly dismissed herself into a closed office. Sebastian wondered where the other residents in the housing building were since he never saw people coming in or out. Then he got a whiff of espresso as Nathaniel released an exaggerated sigh.

"You got here quick," Sebastian said, choosing not to comment on any aspect of Nathaniel's appearance. "Did I pull you away from something?"

Nathaniel scratched his head and darted his eyes to the elevator. "No, just dinner. I'm not hungry, anyway."

"Any chance you've heard from Samara lately? Aria's been looking for her."

Nathaniel took a step back and began moving his lips around while grabbing onto his blazer with both hands. His expression shifted from anxious worry to hopeful excitement. "Wait, were you with Aria just now?"

"Luannie and I went with Aria to look for Samara, but we didn't find her. Then we couldn't find Aria either, and now I can't find Luannie." Sebastian could tell Nathaniel's glossy eyes were trying to keep the unguarded front desk within sight. "Listen, I need you to help me. There must be a way to know where they are. Luannie and I last saw Aria at the campus. She talked in the technology room with Millie, but I don't think she ever came back out, and we couldn't get back in. I want to see everyone accounted for before I go back home."

Nathaniel looked over his shoulder and then marched his way over to the elevator. Sebastian followed.

"I think Millie was upset with Aria," Sebastian added, prompting Nathaniel to press his hand against the elevator door.

Nathaniel inhaled unsteadily and bent the knuckles in his fingers. "Samara has left the program... I've been told four people are no longer with us, including Jaewon, and seeing as you are with me, I would also like to help you locate Aria and Luannie."

Sebastian couldn't stop looking at the side of Nathaniel's face. He saw how messy Nathaniel was and had little trust left in him. Yet, a separate part of himself sensed they would work well together. *Four people?* Sebastian thought, but instead, he asked, "Were you with Millie tonight?"

Nathaniel took a look at his watch, which featured a bright red spot next to the words *<15 meters.* He hit the button to open the elevator door aggressively, making

Sebastian flinch. A smile grew on Nathaniel's face as the door closed between them both. Ignoring Sebastian's question, he said, "I'll get Luannie."

Sebastian hesitantly left the housing building, making eye contact with the staff member at the front desk who had reemerged from the office since Nathaniel dismissed them earlier on. Sebastian briskly walked outside, past Nathaniel's diagonally parked car, and past the small café he never wanted to see again, tired of making the same trips to and from buildings. Sebastian repeated in his mind what Nathaniel had said about going to get Luannie. It gave him hope that Nathaniel was confident about where and how they were, but he didn't let this glimpse of hope get the better of him. He tried opening the other apps on his phone, besides the School of IR, that were used for communication with members in the program. The one that intrigued Sebastian the most was the unnamed app with a photo of a sword and crown.

Sebastian found himself in the center room of the campus building yet again, where a blank television taunted him, and the barely visible door to the technology room beckoned him to take the challenge of trying to get it open. He tried swiping his wrist along the wall, twice, thrice, until he decided to walk to the other side of the room and open the door to the small staircase he had recently climbed with Luannie.

CHAPTER XVII

Nathaniel walked down the hallway on the fourth floor, peeping into the medical room, where he envisioned himself sitting on the edge of the bed with Jaewon not long ago. He looked downcast and pressed his ear up against the door to Luannie's room, where he could hear notifications delivered to a phone. His watch displayed a spot of thermal energy detected in another room just a few feet away from his location. His watch also showed the outline of this figure, its body temperature, heart rate, and breathing pattern.

Nathaniel walked over to the storage room door. He had only been in there once more on the day the scholars first arrived in Sweden. The figure on his watch stopped moving and turned to face Nathaniel on the other side of the door, and its heartbeat accelerated as he swiped his hand to open it. "How did you get in here...?"

Luannie's face flushed, their hair wavier than usual after being let out from Sebastian's braid, and their eyes grew fierce at the sight of Nathaniel.

He glanced at and ignored the materials in their hand. "I'm glad to see you're all right," he offered to Luannie, whose bottom teeth were showing.

They held up a mask with a tube attached that dangled from their fist. "What... is *this*?" One of their eyes squinted, and they abruptly pulled the lid off a box to their right, where there were stored several more masks and tubes. "What... are *these*, and *why* are they not in the medical room with all of the other medical equipment?"

Nathaniel stared at the box full of supplies and noticed Luannie was awaiting an explanation. He opened his mouth to speak when his phone alerted him of a new message. He peered at the screen and ignored an incoming message from Millie.

"How did you know I was in here?" Luannie asked, their neck stretched upward as if to reach Nathaniel's height. "I left my phone in my room."

"I didn't need your phone," Nathaniel responded without further explanation as he hurriedly directed his attention toward a shelf of boxes. He pulled out a stack of paper files when Luannie hissed.

"I've been looking for these!" They grabbed the entire box of the scholars' legal documents and personal information, including their student visas and hand microchip release forms. They flicked through to Jaewon's file and checked under the emergency contact section to confirm that the only language his mother spoke was, in fact, Korean, not English.

Nathaniel was busy opening a second box. He couldn't swallow the lump that had formed in his throat, but he managed to meet Luannie's swollen eyes, knowing they'd been watching. "I have something to tell you."

Nathaniel moved stray strands of hair into place and smoothed over his clothing while Luannie observed. He wanted to ask them to look away while he spoke but didn't. Nathaniel started describing the day they first met at the airport and could imagine the story playing in Luannie's head as they listened.

"I escorted you, Jaewon, and Sebastian from the airport to my car, where one of three drinks in the center cup holder was for each of you. I drove you individually to the housing building and held up fingers to let the front desk receptionist know whether I was arriving with subject number one, two, or three. As we took the elevator to the fourth floor, you were dizzy from the drink I gave you, and I sat you into a chair in the medical room. I quickly strapped down your arms and placed a mask over your mouth and nose to administer anesthesia."

He stopped speaking to shuffle through the box while Luannie's teary eyes focused on the floor. They took a step back when Nathaniel turned to show them three sets of X-rays. He continued to tell the story.

"I hovered a small machine over your head until it latched onto your neck and forehead." He gulped, "It made whirring sounds as it spun in circles."

Luannie barely held onto the evidence Nathaniel handed them. Bringing themself to take a closer look, they analyzed the brain scans and followed the arrows that pointed toward the inner back of the heads, each labeled by name: Luannie, Jaewon, Sebastian.

Nathaniel allowed Luannie to finish visualizing what he had done. "Then, the machine lowered on top of your head and inserted a unique, hair-thin microchip into your brain."

Luannie's chest moved in and out as they heaved, and Nathaniel said nothing more. Luannie touched the top of their head and tried tapping around the spot. They searched around the room with lost eyes before locking back onto Nathaniel's for a brief pause. Nathaniel flinched as they winded their arm backward, swept it around, and aimed out in front of them.

Luannie burst out of the storage room with a few files and ran to their room to grab personal belongings. That's when they noticed the most recent messages from Sebastian on their phone, including an older one from Aria. They threw clothes and accessories hanging from the walls into a bookbag from home, along with important files and documents from the storage room. The School of International Relations tote bag dangled on the knob of a dresser drawer as Luannie left their room for the last time.

"You might be in trouble," Luannie heard Nathaniel say as he stumbled out of the storage room, bloodied around his nose from where they punched him. They bolted for the elevator door at the end of the hall when suddenly it rang out a dinging noise. Somebody was coming up to the fourth floor.

The doors opened, and Luannie released a sigh of relief before running inside the elevator. "Let's go," Luannie said as Nathaniel called something barely audible after the two of them.

The silence was so thick it spilled into the lobby when the elevator door opened, and Luannie emerged with Sebastian, at which the front desk employee became attentive. The two of them made their way outside and crossed the street after Sebastian's lead.

"Do we have to?" Luannie asked in a monotone voice.

"Yeah," Sebastian responded as he interlocked his fingers behind his head. "What's in the bag?"

Luannie flashed a smile, something that felt foreign to them now. "What isn't? I got our visas, passports…" They considered what else to share with him now. "We can try to go back home! I threw in some things from my room too. What about your stuff?"

"Who cares?" Sebastian blurted. He turned to assure Luannie hadn't received his comment the wrong way, but they already knew it wasn't personal. "So, Samara left the program," he stated.

"She went home?" Luannie asked in shock.

"I'm having reservations about believing that myself, but that's what I heard from Nathaniel." Sebastian chose not to share more of what Nathaniel told him about four people leaving the program, including Samara and Jaewon.

On the way to the campus building, Luannie thought about the message they had received from Aria. They didn't have time to read Sebastian's notifications as they scrolled through, but they read the beginning of Aria's. It had said, *Quick,* followed by *please cont—* Luannie remembered driving in Aria's car with Sebastian to the Linnaeus Garden and wondered if they'd get the chance to return someday in the future or if they would want to.

Both Luannie and Sebastian turned their heads toward the street while passing the café to avoid seeing it again, a horrible aspect of the connection they share.

Sebastian hesitated before opening the campus building door. "I'm sorry for leaving you earlier. I was running inhumanely fast circles around this block, and when I stopped, I saw the two of us running around the corner on this side of the street. Millie was there, standing on the sidewalk behind us before getting into her car. I don't know if she saw me, but it was almost too strange to be real. I thought something might've happened to you."

"Something's happened to all of us," Luannie responded. "I went to my room after that to hide and look for our documents Nathaniel collected the day we arrived. We never should've trusted him."

Sebastian didn't inquire further as he entered the campus building.

"I think I could go a while without stepping foot into another elevator again," Luannie remarked out loud.

"Stay here," Sebastian told them as he opened the door near the television and made his way up the staircase. After a few seconds, Luannie could hear his footsteps walking along the floor above them. Sebastian was heading across the lobby, and he stayed there for a minute before traveling just above the technology room. A door clicked open, and Luannie waited for more signs of movement.

"Give me a minute," Luannie heard a voice say behind them. Nathaniel was holding open the front door, his car parked poorly on the street behind him. "You and Sebastian might be in trouble. You need to get out of here."

Luannie squinted their eyes. "You are vile," they hissed, stretching out the words along with their face. They were still trying to distinguish any sounds coming from Sebastian. "We'll be getting out of here without any more of your 'help,'" they said, using quotation marks.

"You don't understand why," Nathaniel insisted.

Luannie responded with explosive laughter. "I haven't asked! What I do know is that Jaewon is dead, Samara supposedly left without notice, and Aria is missing! Save your side of the story. I have a better one." Luannie was interrupted by the sound of furniture moving along the floor in the technology room. They realized Nathaniel noticed the noise, too, and quickly jumped back into their conversation. "The story of how Sebastian and I survive your twisted program."

"It isn't mine," Nathaniel whispered, but at that moment, the door to the technology room slid up into the wall, and there stood Sebastian with a phone in hand.

Sebastian ignored Nathaniel's presence and reached out his arm toward Luannie. "It's hers. This is what I messaged you about earlier." He looked down at the phone screen as he walked over to Luannie's side. "I could hear my messages delivered to Aria earlier, but I couldn't get into the technology room. That staircase," he pointed to the door by the television, "leads to a hall above us here, and it's full of monitors and equipment stamped by the mark of the Swedish Armed Forces. The icon is the same as the unnamed apps on our phones, with the crown and sword on it." He looked at Nathaniel and muttered, "And he didn't want us to see it. Luannie, we need to report this to somebody, all of it, even if they don't believe us. Aria isn't in the technology room, but I saw the furniture moved around. Something might have happened to her. Let's get help." But the uncertainty in his voice as he suggested getting help revealed that the likelihood any authorities would take them seriously was unconvincing.

Luannie felt Sebastian's arm bump into their shoulder as he moved closer. "Nathaniel?" he asked, failing in his attempts to unlock Aria's phone. "Let's start with this. Why exactly did Samara leave the program?"

Nathaniel's bottom lip moved inward, quivering. He gulped and lifted his head and hung it low again. "I'm afraid I've done and said too much to the two of you already."

Sebastian stepped forward again. "What have you done to us already? You haven't told us a thing!" Both of his elbows were bent at his sides, waiting for Nathaniel to elaborate. "What do you know?" Sebastian screamed.

Nathaniel looked like a deer in headlights at the power and grit of Sebastian's voice.

Luannie could see Sebastian seething by the side of his face as they stood behind him. He didn't know yet that he had two microchips—one in his hand and the other in his brain.

"Things weren't supposed to happen like this," Nathaniel whined.

"Sebastian," Luannie approached his side, "we had microchips put into us the day we arrived here, and they're..." They drifted in a search for words, realizing Nathaniel didn't reveal the reason as to why three of the scholars have the chips. "They're in our brains."

Sebastian lifted a hand. Luannie thought to hit Nathaniel, but he lifted it to touch the top of his head.

Luannie continued, "Nathaniel placed them when we each returned from the airport after we drank that beverage in his car. That's why we were all in such a daze the next day." They recalled their anger learning this for the first time and wondered if Sebastian would take it differently coming from them instead of Nathaniel. "You, me, and Jaewon have all been dealing with inexplicable thoughts and feelings since we got here..." They raised their voice and sternly stated, "And it's because of him."

Almost simultaneously, with Luannie pointing their finger at Nathaniel, a loud static came that moved all three of them to hunch over and cover their ears. After a few seconds of disorientation, Luannie turned to face where the pixelated TV screen moved black and white dots around until it formed into a clear, colored video.

A figure on-screen strutted hurriedly down the sidewalk when they slowed to a stop near a parked car. The TV image sharpened, and Luannie could make out the back of the person who now stood near the vehicle. A taller person had stepped outside of the car and seemed to be speaking to the other figure about something urgent as they motioned frantically with their hands. Then, the person at the front of the screen pivoted away from the car and ran down the sidewalk. Her escape encouraged the taller person to get back into their vehicle, and he chased after her.

Out of the corner of Luannie's eye, they noticed Nathaniel back away from the TV.

A young woman ran into a side alley off the city streets, turning behind herself frequently. Luannie couldn't make out her face, but the young woman took a seat and placed her face in her hands, weeping beside a recycling bin. She could hear the sound of a car door in the distance, and a shadow crept into view.

Samara, wearing the same clothes from the meeting with Aria earlier that day, glanced up at the person who had chased her and said, "Please."

There on the screen stood Nathaniel, tall in front of Samara with a briefcase in hand. He checked either end of the ally and also said, "Please..." followed by, "don't make this hard for me." Samara sobbed as Nathaniel removed something Luannie could recognize from his briefcase, a mask and air tube connected to a canister. He applied it to Samara's face as her frightened eyes watched. Then he removed another appliance Luannie recalled hearing about and latched it onto the back of her neck and her forehead. The silver disk made a whirring sound as it lowered over Samara's head, her eyes nearly closed.

Luannie felt tense and wondered what Sebastian was thinking. They could no longer sense Nathaniel standing next to them.

Luannie saw a shadow on the wall behind Samara. The shadow showed Nathaniel remove her Shayla and continue to lower the device over Samara's bare head. Out from the silver rotating disks came down a small tool that descended onto Samara's scalp, made secure placement, and deeply inserted a thin brain microchip.

The TV screen resumed its crackling, and the static was so strong it blurred into a tone capable of deafening someone. Luannie again protected their ears and turned to find Nathaniel squatting against the wall, crying similarly to how Samara sobbed in the city alleyway. The static drastically lowered, and the outline of a new figure appeared on the screen this time.

"Hello..." a familiar voice spoke in an upbeat tone like that of a university alumnus welcoming prospective students. Nova removed her specs and stood surrounded by all sorts of gadgets. She laughed when Sebastian looked up at the ceiling where the small staircase connected to the technology room. "What are you peeping at, Sebastian? You know I'm not up there," she clarified, her brown eyes shining on the screen. "No, I'm at work! And I'd like for you all to come visit me. Now," she advised, smiling wide enough to flash her set of perfectly aligned teeth. "And Nathaniel," her voice sang, "Millie asks that you bring her some food since she wasn't able to eat after you left her alone at dinner."

Luannie looked at the message Aria had sent to them and then longingly toward the technology room. "Quick, please contact Nathaniel and the authorities. Millie has told me she—"

CHAPTER XVIII

Sebastian looked between the two headrests in front of him and through the car's front windshield, his lips crumpled in anger. Nathaniel's car had completely tinted windows from the outside so nobody could distinguish anything inside, but Sebastian could see everything crystal clear from the inside out. Sebastian wanted to speak with Luannie, who sat on his left, but he feared Nathaniel would overhear their conversation or become suspicious.

Sebastian typed a message to show Luannie without pressing send on his phone. The statement read *He put microchips in our brains? Should we take over the car?*

Luannie cleared their throat lightly and also began typing a message for Sebastian on their phone. It read *I don't think Nathaniel is holding up too well. Look at him.* Nathaniel wiped tears away from his cheek and continued driving faster than the speed limit. They shrugged at Sebastian and stared at the back of Nathaniel's head.

"Are you two talking about me?" Nathaniel asked, his voice wavering.

"Maybe," Sebastian said, refraining from saying more.

"We'd talk directly to you, but we don't know how to feel about somebody who lied to us about Samara and placed microchips in our brains," Luannie added. "Where is she now, anyway?"

Nathaniel sighed and sat upright. He patted his briefcase that sat on the passenger seat. "Take it."

Sebastian grabbed the briefcase and tried to pry it open, but the screen that sealed it shut had an eight-digit code required to unlock it.

"Manually," Nathaniel said.

Sebastian looked at the front of the briefcase, where there was a place to enter a code on a digital screen, scan a microchip, or scroll eight number dials. Sebastian figured Nathaniel meant to use the third method.

"Two, seventeen, fifteen, thirty-one, four, twenty-five, five, forty," Nathaniel said as Sebastian scrolled to each number.

The briefcase popped open, and Sebastian met Nathaniel's eyes in the rearview mirror. Those weren't the same cold blue eyes he saw the night Millie chased after him and Luannie. Luannie instantly searched the contents of the briefcase. Inside was a tiny, empty container, a brain scan labeled "Samara," a device like Nathaniel used on Samara, and underneath a brain diagram with microchip placement instructions. At the bottom were letters addressed to Nova from a confidential sender.

Nathaniel's hand stretched backward between Sebastian and Luannie. He motioned his hand for them to place something in his palm, and after a brief pause, Luannie smacked down their phone. Nathaniel abruptly pulled over and immediately got to work on removing the SIM card that the scholars received when they first got their phones. He reached his hand back again for Sebastian's and took out his SIM card as well.

"What you're looking at in the briefcase is what I used to place a brain microchip in Samara earlier today. I regret to inform you I cannot confirm her whereabouts or well-being. I followed an order to place the brain microchip, which is the extent of my knowledge on the matter. You all know Nova." He paused for a response before continuing. "A little more than a year ago, she received funding to research brain microchips' impact on animals, which expanded to include Homo sapiens. Ever since everyone in Sweden has been getting chips in their hands, Nova and her higher-ups believe chips in our brains would be the next big thing."

Luannie removed a few papers from the briefcase to read while Sebastian listened attentively to Nathaniel. He began driving again, no longer as animated as he usually was.

"Millie and I have worked for Chipd over the past five years since its creation. It's where we met. Our relationship with Nova is that she employed us to find a diverse group of young adults to volunteer to have her brain microchip prototypes tested on them. Of course, we couldn't think of anyone, and that's when a friend of Nova's gave us an idea. The friend wanted her daughter to be involved with the breakthrough, a pioneer of the development of brain microchips."

"How selfish," Sebastian said. "If Nova's friend wanted to make her daughter famous, she should have only placed a microchip in her."

Nathaniel shifted himself in his seat and softened his pressure on the gas pedal. "You saw me place one in her earlier today."

Luannie looked up from the papers in their hand.

"Samara's mother does business throughout Europe, but what Samara never knew was that her mother funds several technology projects that trace back to Chipd Headquarters," Nathaniel revealed. "On the bright side, this means Samara is most likely fine."

Sebastian watched the other cars whip by from the window and wondered where Nathaniel was taking them. "Samara doesn't know her mother created this program?"

Nathaniel leaned back into his seat. "Well, not exactly."

Sebastian scoffed and looked at Luannie, who continued reading letters from Nathaniel's briefcase.

"Samara doesn't know her mother recommended her as a volunteer, but she knows what the program involves. However, none of us know why the program involves what it does. That's why I have that briefcase." Nathaniel pointed behind him and caught Luannie scanning their eyes over the letters. "I printed those from Nova's laptop. I'm not sure what they say exactly. Some of the text is in code."

Sebastian rested an elbow on Luannie's shoulder and joined them in reading the content of the messages, which were emails sent back and forth between Nova and another person.

After a few minutes of silence, Nathaniel continued speaking. "Samara accepted the opportunity, but she started to get cold feet, especially since she was advised not to disclose any information, including her family. Samara didn't want to be one of the first volunteers to test a Chipd brain microchip anymore. At the time, Nova reported that her higher-ups were getting impatient and needed subjects from various backgrounds by the end of the year. That's when Samara suggested we create the School of International Relations."

Sebastian opened his mouth to say something, but Luannie grabbed his arm in the form of silent protest. Sebastian retreated, focusing again on the messages in their laps.

"Nobody was supposed to get hurt. The messages you're reading—"

"We see them," Luannie interrupted and began to read aloud. "...Push a person's breaking points... Personalized experiences. Testing subjects on their physical pain thresholds undetected, without altering the health of the brain..." Luannie huffed. "We are not subjects," they demanded, this time prompting Sebastian to grab onto their arm.

"This is only an experiment!" Nathaniel raised his voice. "It was supposed to be exciting."

"Exciting for who, exactly? You knew it was wrong enough to keep it a secret. You designed a fake school to carry out this plan," Luannie said, gripping tightly onto the edges of the piece of paper in their hand.

"Well," Nathaniel said weakly, pushing his lips to the side. "It's not like we didn't know that not acquiring consent was legally or morally wrong, but Nova felt pressed to start, and thus Millie and I were as well. It's ironic. Samara's mother wanted Samara involved as one of the first people to test a Chipd brain microchip, but with how things worked out, she didn't need to get one. Her job in the International Scholars program was to be our plant. Samara arrived here earlier than all of you in preparation for the experiment, and she was here when you spoke together on *Connected* for us to listen in on the meeting. Any guilt about recruiting other people her age for the experiment disappeared when she realized what she was avoiding." Nathaniel took a break before saying, "What she never counted on was Jaewon's passing. She wasn't the same after that."

"Neither are we," Sebastian remarked.

The car was quiet for about thirty minutes as Nathaniel allowed time for Luannie and Sebastian to register the information he had shared with them. Their destination was about an hour from campus, and time was moving quickly.

Sebastian had difficulty digesting how elaborate this scheme he and Luannie found themselves in, and he thought about life back home for comfort. He wanted to meditate with his mom, play soccer with his friends from high school, visit his father at his new job, or attend a legitimate university.

Luannie folded a few pieces of paper from Nathaniel's briefcase and stuck them into their book bag.

"Fifteen minutes," Nathaniel alerted them. "I need to speak with Millie when we arrive at Chipd."

"Then you might want to put on your ring," Sebastian suggested with a smirk.

Nathaniel wiggled the band out of his pocket and returned it onto his left ring finger in disgust. "I know neither of you has a reason to trust me, but I would like to make up for the irreversible damage in which I've been complicit." When he didn't receive a response, he shared more. "Millie and I were on the tenth floor of Chipd Headquarters, where Mattias Rozelle, a fellow junior engineer, worked before Nova agreed to join forces with him. Last year, the Swedish Armed Forces were all over Chipd Headquarters, scoping out the employees following the emergence of widespread hand microchip use. They needed to ensure the production was on the up and up." He gnawed at a fingernail. "There's hope for me still. I can return to my old job and be sound of mind and away from this project. Alive."

Sebastian wasn't sure if he thought Nathaniel deserved to get out of this situation well-off or alive. He still didn't understand why the brain microchips needed to test human mental and physical pain levels. Still, Sebastian was more concerned with how they would get back home, with the program directors aware of how much they knew already. Then he remembered that Luannie had all their documents in their possession now.

"What does Nova want with us?" Sebastian asked.

"Your minds," Nathaniel answered without missing a beat. "She wants to analyze your brains over time and how they react to certain stimuli, how you handle the challenges she throws at you, how you maneuver between a blend of pretend and reality. But she needs to know you personally first, which is why having Samara get to know you all came in handy." Nathaniel looked over his shoulder and eyed his briefcase that remained in Sebastian's lap. "I need something from out of there. Every printed email needs to stay behind. There should be a brain scan with today's date labeled with Samara's name within those papers. That can stay in the briefcase, as well as the device, instructions, and empty microchip container."

"Why should we hand the printed messages to you after everything you just admitted to?" Sebastian questioned, waiting for Nathaniel's justification. "We could take the entire briefcase and run."

Nathaniel chuckled lightly. "You wouldn't make it very far." He tapped on the top of his head. "You're in trouble with or without me here, but Millie and Nova aren't going to offer you help anytime soon. Millie has expressed no remorse since the beginning of this mess, and Nova has only been finding it more and more amusing." Nathaniel pivoted in his seat to look at them while stopped at a traffic light. "I want to help the two of you return home without being manipulated to literal death." Nathaniel became emotional again, and Sebastian wondered whether he truly felt guilty or had prior experience in performing arts before his job as a tenth-floor junior engineer. "I don't know what Nova wants from you today or what she'd try to do, but I honestly believe the success of your test runs is too important for her to ruin, especially since she's already down one after losing Jaewon."

Sebastian saw the words "Chipd Headquarters" on a silver and white twelve-story building they approached. He nodded to Luannie, and they compiled the printed messages from Nathaniel's briefcase, all except for the ones Luannie slipped into their bag.

"Your evidence," Sebastian said, scrambling the number scrolls and slamming the briefcase down on the passenger seat of the car.

Nathaniel parked, unbuckled himself, and turned around to face Sebastian and Luannie in the backseat again. "Unless someone logs into your accounts and shuts down your microchips, Nova will be able to continue manipulating you however she wants. I couldn't find how to do it on her laptop before, so I will try again while we're in here."

The three of them walked across the main lobby of Chipd Headquarters, which still ran partially as a hand microchip administration site. They passed a line that contained hundreds of people who snaked across the floor in a winding file that made the best use of space.

"Looks like you're going to have to step onto another elevator sooner than you'd hoped," Sebastian joked to Luannie. They couldn't manage a compelling chuckle, so he didn't push for one.

Nathaniel pressed the button for the second-lowest laboratory floor at Chipd, but nothing happened. "Oh," he said foolishly, "I forgot." He swiped his hand and gained access to the floor that belonged to Nova's laboratory.

"And you had to agree to come here. Why?" Luannie asked Nathaniel as they descended.

"I can't just up and leave. I have too much invested here still, too many loose ends to attend. The two of you still have a chance at returning to your freedom. The freedom I want back is in the same place I lost it," Nathaniel explained. "Here." He pointed to the elevator button for floor ten.

"*Labb, nivå två*, lab level two," a monotone voice announced as the elevator door opened on the second-lowest laboratory floor at Chipd.

Sebastian stared in awe at several rows of tables, all covered in microchip samples, lining the path to a small space where Nova stood waiting for them to walk in. Nova tapped a code into the air before her, and Sebastian watched in awe as an electronic shield crackled into view and powered off. The contents that surrounded Nova were visible when peeping into the entrance of the room at an angle. Thousands of gadgets were labeled in a series of barely visible numbers, letters, and symbols in air-tight condensed rows.

"Don't be shy; come on in! I'd love to see the International Scholars again," Nova exclaimed without a hint of detectable sarcasm.

Nathaniel walked around Luannie and Sebastian and through the many appliances to where Nova stood to greet them. Nathaniel turned around and motioned for them to join. Luannie began strutting down the path, and Sebastian, hesitant at first, followed behind. He felt uneasy as a Cheshire smile crept onto Nova's face.

"Oh, it's so nice to see you both again," Nova said. "You just missed Millie," she directed toward Nathaniel. "She had to leave about ten minutes ago, on an empty stomach." She winked. "You can drop off what I asked for on a table over there." Nova pointed to a small room on the wall to her right.

Nathaniel gave Sebastian and Luannie a stiff upper lip smile before leaving them.

Nova's eyes followed Nathaniel to the room and then laid upon Luannie. "Well! My two scholars." She scrunched up her smile with the rest of her face. "I've heard that you've heard things." Nova stared with wide eyes and giggled.

"Seen and felt things too," Luannie added.

"Ah, yes. What is the human existence if not experienced by the senses we possess?" Nova proposed.

Sebastian rolled his eyes, but Nova didn't see because she walked deeper into her workroom.

"Why don't you take a look at something?" she invited Luannie and Sebastian.

Sebastian stepped up first this time, his head turning every which way to take in the atmosphere. He watched as Nova grabbed two small containers. Each looked similar to the one Nathaniel kept in his briefcase. She held them in her upward palms and extended toward Sebastian and Luannie for them to see.

"Do you know the difference between these two microchips?" Nova asked, looking between the two of them.

"Is one for a hand and one for a brain?" Luannie asked,
their voice devoid of all enthusiasm.

"Oh? No, these are two hand microchip prototypes that
differ only in tiny but significant details," she said with
emphasis on her adjectives. "Although you are right to
assume that I have brain microchips as well, Luannie."
Nova returned the two containers to their designated
area and located another two containers. "And how about
these?" she asked, looking at Sebastian.

"I can't tell by just looking at them. Are one for an animal
and another for a human?" he asked.

Nova raised her eyebrows. "Interesting guesses, you two.
Yes, I have also created microchips for other animals. But
these two are," she shrugged, "rather special."

Sebastian shifted by the way Nova spoke as if there was
a shared secret about her work.

"You see, the one in my left hand is a brain microchip, and
the one in my right a hand microchip. Most have a certain
amount of storage space to maintain all the information it
calculates. But these have less storage space than the average chips for these prototypes because they have already
had data downloaded from prior use." Nova handed the
containers to Luannie, and they grabbed them without
giving Nova the satisfaction of an emotional response.

"If you put a used hand microchip into another subject, they will have access to everything the microchip was programmed to access. However, if you put a used brain microchip into another subject, it would create serious altercations in the new subject," Nova explained.

Sebastian moved his weight onto the other foot and waited for Luannie to pass him the chip containers Nova had handed them. Luannie noticed his gaze and placed them into his hands.

"You might also find these specific chips interesting because these were the ones used in a previous subject that you observed. Jaewon," Nova said, her eyes like daggers into Sebastian's, then into Luannie's.

Sebastian's grip on the containers tightened, and Luannie's nostrils flared.

"Everything there was to know about Jaewon? It's all in there." Nova pointed to the containers in Sebastian's hands. "The both of you have your very own, unique brain microchip too. They store so much information about yourselves that you may not even know! You can use them to improve your cognitive functions, emotional intelligence, and physical capabilities. Is there anything that either of you has always wanted to improve in?"

Luannie huffed out of their nose, and Sebastian looked over to Nathaniel, whose briefcase sat on the floor while he frantically typed on a laptop in the other room.

"Patience," Sebastian said calmly. "I didn't realize how much room for improvement there was until being pushed to my limits." He ignored Luannie's glance.

"Very good! The best part is, we don't know if you've reached your limit, if you've even gotten close, or if it's been moving higher to withstand more adversity. You are incredibly strong-willed, Sebastian. Stubborn, even. And that has helped you so far. But when I poke at your weaknesses, your fears, you struggle to control yourself. That's something you need to learn to be aware of as it's happening." Nova faced her body toward Luannie now. "How about you, Luannie? Anything you think you should or would like to improve on?"

Luannie shared a few rapid blinks to keep their eyes from drying. "As Sebastian said, there's so much room for improvement..."

Nova lowered her brows and let a smirk slide into her cheek, where a deep dimple formed. "I haven't gathered much information on you yet, Luannie, and I look forward to working with you more," Nova said, turning her back to the scholars. "When the two of you leave here today, you will leave here with both of your chips still in place."

Sebastian and Luannie both shot each other a quick set of concerned expressions.

"They will stay there until the completion of your trials, and then Nathaniel or I will remove your brain microchip," Nova said. Then she whispered into a watch on her wrist. "Time to come back, crybaby." Nova's voice spoke in the room where Nathaniel stood.

Nathaniel entered the room and stood beside Luannie. "Everything is going well in here?"

"Mattias, Jaewon, Samara, Aria... I would hate for anyone else to have to leave our program," she told Nathaniel.

His face turned pale at hearing Aria's name.

"Nathaniel," she started, "Luannie and Sebastian here are now aware of their experiential importance and understand they will have their brain microchips removed upon the success of the project."

Nova was no longer all smiles.

"The two of you are brave, smart, strong..." she said to the scholars in an uplifting tone. "But your progress is little to none, I'm afraid. I need to measure your progress, so half-hearted efforts aren't going to help because half-hearted efforts are what the average person already performs in the face of adversity. You have a choice." Nova turned around to resume her work. "And, Nathaniel, let's not tell our scholars here so much about things they don't understand. No need to get them all confused." She didn't see, but Nathaniel nodded in agreement. "You may leave," she dismissed them.

Nathaniel motioned with his head for Sebastian and Luannie to follow him to the elevator. They all speed-walked in collective silence, and just as Nathaniel was about to press the button to open the elevator door, Nova cleared her throat at the end of the path lined by microchip tables.

"You may leave, but not before giving me back Jaewon's chips, Sebastian." She grew a gruesome smile and extended her arm out with palm face up the entire time Sebastian walked back to her by himself. When he placed them into her hand, her fingers recoiled. She recoiled too, back into her room, with the electromagnetic field crackling as it turned on again.

Sebastian joined Nathaniel and Luannie in the elevator and stared at the back of Nova's head as she put Jaewon's microchips away. He swore she could have sensed him watching because she peeked an eye over her shoulder as the door closed shut.

CHAPTER XIX

Walking through the main lobby of Chipd Headquarters, Luannie overheard a microchip placer speaking with somebody who had asked about having her chip paused and reactivated in the future.

"All updates to the chips can be done online through Chipd administrators without physically accessing the chip itself unless a new prototype is released. In that case, the old chip would be removed and replaced with the latest version," he ensured while looking down at her hand.

The woman's voice shook as she asked, "Can you tell me when it is about to go in, please? I do best with a warning."

He smiled and looked up at her, "I already did it while explaining the answer to your previous question. As we say, it's a fast, minimally invasive procedure not many find painful. You're all chipped!"

She laughed and gathered her belongings to allow the next person to sit, and the snake line inched forward.

As Luannie ducked into the car, Nathaniel leaned against the front door. Sebastian was about to join Luannie in the backseat, but he walked around the car and leaned against Luannie's door, besides a devolving Nathaniel. Nobody had eaten a full meal all day, and Nathaniel's demeanor was no longer as upbeat as usual. He rubbed his eyes and supported the back of his neck with interlocked fingers, looking up at the not-completely-set Swedish summer sun.

"Luannie and I need to get home," Sebastian said, ignoring his stomach growl. He turned to face the side of Nathaniel's head, admiring the outline of his intense nose and sharp jawline. "And *you* need to get back to floor ten."

Nathaniel smiled and met Sebastian's eyes, searching for sincerity. He tried to wipe off scuff marks on his left shoe with his right. "Do I?" Nathaniel left the rhetorical question to sit on their minds before getting into the car.

Luannie pursed their lips at Sebastian as he got in, having heard their conversation, and he responded with a shrug. Luannie rolled their eyes and clutched onto their book bag.

"Did you take anything from in there?" Sebastian asked.

"No, but nice try holding onto Jaewon's chips," Luannie said.

"Keeping the physical chips is not merely for her memorabilia or the symbol of scientific achievement. She needs them to access his information," Nathaniel informed them both as he set his briefcase on the passenger seat. Realizing this insight did not amuse the scholars, he added, "She won't be able to access Sebastian's any longer. I was able to stop the program connected to your brain microchip and change its password."

Sebastian shared an open-mouthed smile, but Luannie's was small as they congratulated him. Sebastian gathered himself and wrapped an arm around Luannie. "He'll do the same for you as soon as he can," he reassured them. "Won't you?" he asked Nathaniel.

Nathaniel nodded and pulled away from the curb.

The car ride was fifteen minutes of silence toward the same direction as the housing building. Luannie recognized this and figured Sebastian did too, but neither mentioned it. They intently scanned the city surroundings through the window, looking for signs in case they needed to tell someone of their location.

Nathaniel was stopped at a red light when he announced they would be stopping within the next five minutes. "I would like to help you return home. Luannie, I trust you held onto your visas, passports, and IDs?" He checked for their nod. "But all Nova has to do is tap into your brain microchips and prevent you from boarding a plane."

Luannie hadn't considered that Nova could keep them in Sweden and that they could lose their complete bodily autonomy at any moment. "So, we chance it," they spoke up. "She can't keep us in one spot!"

Nathaniel explained, "Microchips won't fall out of range while you're flying overseas. No matter where you go, Nova will be able to complete her experiment with you. If you challenge her, she may make your lives miserable or push you to the point she did with Jaewon or Samara. She can make you do anything."

Luannie groaned with eyes full of fear and looked out of the window. They remembered what Nova had said about how she or Nathaniel would remove their microchips at the end of the project's completion. "You can do it," Luannie said, looking outside at the cars passing by. "Take out our chips."

Nathaniel parted his lips, and Sebastian scooted up between the two front seats.

"Yeah! You put them in, so you can take them out for us. You want to help us return home, right?" Sebastian reminded him.

Nathaniel quietly slowed to a park outside of a modern, red-walled hotel. "Will you two please stay here a moment? I need to take care of something."

Sebastian rolled his eyes and leaned back into the seat next to Luannie. "Meeting with someone?" he asked.

"Hey. I'll only be a few minutes," Nathaniel told Sebastian from outside the car before slamming the door shut.

"How much do you want to bet he's going in there to end things with Millie right now?" Sebastian asked Luannie with a smile.

Luannie stared blankly at his face until his smile disappeared. They opened their bag and rummaged through its contents, first pulling out the brain scans identified as theirs and Sebastian's. Next, they removed Jaewon's file and opened it to the page that included primary personal contact information for his relative in case of an emergency. "For all we know, Millie could end Nathaniel," Luannie suggested, pointing out the language spoken by Jaewon's mother.

Sebastian remembered hearing Jaewon talk about his family and how Millie spoke to his mother after his passing. He felt his bottom lip begin to quiver. "Do you think his mom even knows?"

Luannie didn't engage in that thought as their eyes scanned one of the messages they took from Nathaniel's briefcase. It was addressed to Nova and appeared to be written by a confidential business partner.

Sebastian looked outside to see if Nathaniel was on his way back before leaning closer and peeping over Luannie's shoulder to read the message.

"Well, what's it say, Luannie?" he strained his voice impatiently.

"Who would advise something like this?" they muttered under their breath after a minute and brought it closer between themself and Sebastian so he could see the words more clearly. "This order describes torture. Sebastian... I think this project is funded by... terrorists?" Their statement converted into a question as they said it aloud. "Look at this," they said and pointed out words on the paper that read: "Overwhelming to the point of debilitating any potential opponents."

Sebastian also spotted a shocking grouping of words to point out, which read: *Trial runs must guarantee results of deceased persons to gather accurate measurements of the strategies utilized.*

"What the hell does this—?" Sebastian left his sentence incomplete at the sight of Millie emerging from the exit revolving door of the hotel lobby. "Millie," he said. "Put those away," he told Luannie.

Millie was walking directly toward Nathaniel's car with a smirk growing on her smug face. Sebastian lowered his head to see her entire frame coming toward them, and she arched an eyebrow. She was within three feet of Luannie's side door when she diverted across the street to her parked car.

Sebastian's eyes grew. "Nathaniel!" He jumped out of the car and jogged to the revolving door entrance without a plan when Nathaniel came through.

"Come on!" Nathaniel invited Sebastian to glide with him to his car without taking a look up at where Millie stood by hers, glaring at the two of them.

Sebastian watched Millie from inside Nathaniel's car as she drove away and recognized her eyes piercing him through her rearview mirror, the same as she had the other night.

Nathaniel pulled out onto the road and said, "Get your passports ready." He turned on the radio as they drove away, and Sebastian recognized the song that was playing. It was a song that sounded like a cross between techno, rock, and Frank Sinatra.

"Hey, I've heard this before," said Sebastian.

"Yeah?" Nathaniel said, perking up. "I love this song."

Recalling where he had first heard it, he asked softly, "Do you miss Aria at all?"

Nathaniel gripped the steering wheel and looked over at the briefcase on his passenger seat. "Of course, I do. Aria was a personal friend of mine. We met in college, and I was the one who hired her to work at the School of International Relations. Such a bubbly person, perfect for university," he thought aloud. His smile faded as his fondness of Aria reminded him of recent events.

"Are you sure she's gone?" Luannie asked.

Nathaniel nodded his head and ran his fingers through his hair, no ring present on his ring finger. "Millie just confirmed that for me."

After twenty minutes of riding on the highway further in the direction of Uppsala, Luannie spotted a sign for the international Stockholm Arlanda Airport. They went to tell Sebastian, but something prevented them from looking to their left. A concerned expression on Luannie's face froze in place, and they couldn't bring themself to vocalize their circumstance. Luannie's eyes could only see as far as the side of Nathaniel's head in the front seat.

A truck was facing the wrong direction on the highway, and Luannie watched it through the front windshield with their head at a forty-five-degree angle toward the window, their limbs where they had been when they first saw the sign for the airport. No amount of pressure allowed Luannie to make noise, and the truck's front only appeared to be getting closer and closer on the highway. They saw another airport sign, but when they read it, the sign abruptly flipped around to face oncoming traffic, and the muscles in their eyes tensed as they tried to widen them.

Luannie was hoping Nathaniel would ask a question and realize something was wrong. They looked between Nathaniel's head and the truck heading toward them. Then, two arms went flailing in front of them.

Sebastian watched in horror as Luannie wrapped their fingers around Nathaniel's throat.

The car swerved on the road, prompting neighboring cars to honk excessively. Nathaniel's right hand gripped the steering wheel while his left tried to pry Luannie's fingers off of him. Sebastian called Luannie's name and bent their arms at the elbows, forcing them to loosen their grip on Nathaniel's throat. The airport was in sight as Nathaniel increased his speed and leaned as far forward in his seat as he could. Sebastian finally held onto Luannie's hands as Nathaniel took a deep inhale, struggling to regain a regular breathing pattern.

"Luannie," Sebastian said sternly, looking at their eyes but unable to look into them. "Hey." He looked between Nathaniel and Luannie and decided to keep a hold of their hands for the time being.

"You need to do something, Nathaniel. We can't have them on a plane like this!" he shouted.

The car pulled into the furthermost parking spot in the airport garage, screeching to a halt, and Nathaniel fumbled to scan his microchip to unlock his briefcase. The only item that remained was what he used to place the brain microchip into Samara.

"Okay, okay," he said to himself. "Okay, I've only practiced microchip removal on a model, but—"

"What?" Sebastian asked in disbelief.

"It's a lot different than removing a hand microchip," Nathaniel responded in self-defense. "And I don't have any more medicine… I can try to remove it now, but Luannie would have to remain completely still." Nathaniel's hands were shaking as he looked at Luannie, who was present physically but not mentally as they struggled to regain control over themselves.

"*You* need to stay still, man," Sebastian told him, eyeing his trembling hands.

"Right, right. I know. I just…" Nathaniel prepared his equipment to extract the brain microchip and motioned with his hand for Sebastian to move Luannie into the center of the backseat.

A few more cars entering into the garage distracted Sebastian, but then he remembered Nathaniel's car windows tinted from the outside. *How could Millie see Luannie and me earlier? She must have assumed we were with Nathaniel.*

Luannie's head jerked side to side, and their eyes intensified, focusing on Nathaniel's face.

"You need to do it now!" Sebastian insisted.

Nathaniel faced the backseat and reached over Luannie's head, carefully lowering the machine over their scalp, latching it to their forehead and back of their neck. It whirred as silver rings spun, and a small piece descended closer to Luannie's hair. Nathaniel felt around until locating the correct location and repositioned his machine.

"Okay," he whispered teary-eyed, releasing the thin tool through Luannie's skin and into their brain. The car was silent as Nathaniel navigated the area, looking to hold onto the microchip firmly and swiftly retrieve it.

Sebastian watched in awe as Nathaniel saw the inside of Luannie's head on the machine's screen. Sebastian steadied himself as Nathaniel seemed to get a grip on the microchip piece.

"Do you have it?" Sebastian barely spoke, afraid to divert Nathaniel's attention away from the procedure. The thin tool carefully lifted out from Luannie's scalp with a tiny microchip held onto its end within less than ten seconds.

Sebastian grinned and laid a hand on Nathaniel's shoulder. They shared a moment of relief before Nathaniel's briefcase sounded a few beeps, as if an alarm had gone off.

"Oh, dear," Nathaniel said.

"Oh, dear, what?" Sebastian asked, holding Luannie's head up to prevent it from flopping sideways.

"The code for my briefcase. I scanned it with my microchip instead of opening it manually this time," Nathaniel said, but Sebastian stared at him blankly. Nathaniel explained, "Nova can see when I access the briefcase this way."

Luannie murmured groggily beside Sebastian when Nathaniel's phone began ringing.

He slid it out of his pocket and answered reluctantly, holding a finger over his lips to Sebastian and Luannie.

"Nova," he greeted her neutrally.

"It seems as though Sebastian's brain microchip is disabled, and I cannot access his account. Any idea why that may be?" she asked.

"Hmm, well, he certainly seemed to understand what you told him about his role in your experiment. Perhaps he is now performing far better than you predicted he could, exceeding your expectations," Nathaniel suggested, half-serious, half-sarcastic. "Or, perhaps, there is a glitch on your laptop or some other technical malfunction... There must be an explanation."

There was silence on the other end of the phone. "Yes, I'm sure there must."

Nathaniel checked out the car window to watch as other cars arrived for their flights. He rubbed his eyes and let out a loud yawn, inspiring one from Sebastian.

"Have you accessed your Chipd briefcase recently? What was the situation?" Nova asked.

"Ah, yes, I have. I needed to make sure I left all the necessary documents in your lab earlier," Nathaniel said.

"That's something you should've ensured before you left here." Nova's tone switched. "I couldn't help but notice your current location, Nathaniel."

Nathaniel was silent. Then he tilted his head. "Mine? Chipd placed my microchip, but only the Public Health Agency and Swedish Armed forces have access to my location."

"Well, the hand chips I gave to Luannie and Sebastian are both out of range on my watch. Care to say hello for me?" And with that, Nova ended the call.

Nathaniel watched Luannie blink their tired eyes open. "You two have to go now. Go inside the airport and show them your documents—Luannie has them. Ask for the soonest flights back home, and ask someone to make a call to someone you know back home if you need to." Nathaniel backed up into his seat, manually opened his briefcase to put away his device, and shuffled through his wallet. "Here, this should be more than enough for the two of you to eat dinner in the food court, pay for your flights, and hire a cab wherever you land." He looked at Luannie, who was looking back at him, trying to hang onto his every word.

Sebastian took a moment to collect himself before turning away from Nathaniel and helping Luannie out of the car with their belongings.

Nathaniel met them outside. "I'm... I know this wasn't..." He couldn't form a complete thought. "I don't know what else to say. I'm glad you two are well and on your way home now. I don't know what will become of me, but that's my bed to lay in." He shrugged and offered a small smile.

Sebastian's lips slowly turned upward until he was also smiling, which was against what his mind told him he should do. "I'll never forget this," Sebastian said in a stern voice.

Nathaniel bowed his head in guilt, and Sebastian added, "I couldn't if I tried." He backed away, fighting the urge to either hug or hit Nathaniel, and turned around with Luannie under his left arm. He walked to the other end of the garage until taking one last look at Nathaniel behind him, who rose a hand into the air like Sebastian's father had when he left Brazil.

Sebastian walked with Luannie into the airport, and he noticed everyone using their microchips to access ATMs, booking confirmations, and vending machine orders. As he glanced at a news report on the television screen confirming the expansion of hand microchips to neighboring countries, his phone received a notification for a file that had airdropped from a nearby device. Sebastian checked his surroundings before clicking on it, which opened to a photo album from the day they took a trip to the Royal Palace in Stockholm. He swiped through them with glassy eyes and thought, *I'll text these to Luannie once we use our old phone numbers again.*

Nathaniel walked around the back of his car and entered the driver's seat. He cracked his knuckles before speeding out of the parking lot and getting back onto the highway. He scanned his hand over the dashboard, and the song Aria showed him resumed on the radio as he passed a sign for Uppsala. Nathaniel pressed a few buttons on the dashboard until the phone rang.

"Nathaniel," Nova said, surprised that he initiated a call.

"I'm on my way to you now. Let's meet back where we started, and make sure Millie is there too."

CHAPTER XX

FIVE MONTHS LATER

Nathaniel walked through the empty lobby of Chipd Headquarters, where a newscaster on a television screen reported in Swedish: "Within a year and a half of its creation, nine-tenths of the Swedish population now possess Chipd's hand microchip. We now face the challenge of rapidly continuing to upgrade technology in every aspect of life. Doing so also means Chipd may design a new microchip with advanced capabilities to match our future needs. Chipd is already planning its expansion with business partners in neighboring countries looking to adopt the technology."

Nathaniel swiped his way onto the elevator and rose to the tenth floor with a content smile. The door slid open, and he greeted fellow junior engineers with whom he was familiar. His old desk was clear, boxes full of his belongings on the floor and chair. As he placed the last few items from his cubicle into a box, he paused to look at the School of International Relations logo design drafts from a few months earlier in a stack of loose papers. Nathaniel put them into the box and then picked up a printed photo underneath of him and a younger woman. The image was dated eight years beforehand and featured Nathaniel and Aria at their college graduation in caps and gowns. His eyes wandered around his old workspace and around the other workers on the floor, and then he quickly finished throwing the rest of his items into the box while keeping a professional composure.

"Nathaniel!" a deep, celebratory voice called. "Let's get a move on." The man with light hair moved Nathaniel along and carried a few boxes over to the elevator door.

Nathaniel grabbed his remaining boxes and joined the Commander in Chief of the Swedish Armed Forces on the elevator, granting access to land on the second-lowest basement floor. "I appreciate your help, Erik. I thought I may never step foot in this building again."

"Ha!" Erik laughed. "Why not? My correspondence with Nova never led to the creation of an organized team for this project. You're not only a strong worker independently; you're a team leader. Now it's time to start thinking like the superintendent you are..." The door slid open to a renovated version of Nova's old lab, "in your new laboratory."

"*Labb, nivå två,* lab level two," a monotone voice announced as the elevator door opened on the second-lowest laboratory floor at Chipd.

Nathaniel walked into an open space with new working tables, each designated for an individual junior engineer. Tables lined the left wall with brain models and utensils, and along the right wall were work and meeting spaces. "I have my first meeting with the team tomorrow," he said, leading Erik toward the back of the room. He touched the air before him in a specific pattern until an electric current crackled and unlocked the invisible field that once protected Nova and her work. "I'm glad I'll still be able to work with some of my old coworkers. They're all brilliant and committed to our mission."

Erik entered the room, the interior of which was only visible from the inside. Microchip prototypes for animals and humans, hands and brains, were stacked on all walls. On the wall above Nathaniel's main laptop was a double container that housed Jaewon's used microchips. Nathaniel acknowledged them and unlocked his laptop with a scan of his hand.

"Where are our old friends?" Erik grinned.

"Right here," Nathaniel said, unlocking a series of camera footage aimed in different angles toward eight chairs in the center of the campus building's technology room. Two women sat strapped in the center-most chairs with their heads beneath a larger version of Nathaniel's microchip placement device. The device hovered over each chair but only connected to Nova and Millie's heads.

"They are currently undergoing one of our latest tests," Nathaniel informed Erik. Nathaniel pulled up a screen that tracked Nova and Millie's health statistics through the Public Health Agency, access granted to him by the Swedish Armed Forces, and another screen that measured the success of their abilities in the brain test they were taking. "Nova is performing significantly better than Millie, likely because she is familiar with aspects of the original program. But I will meet our newest subjects this weekend when they arrive to fill our remaining six seats. The entire second floor of campus is ready for our second run. And after speaking with your friend, the receptionist at the housing building, the scholars will have access to reside on the third and fourth floors."

"Perfect," Erik whispered in delight, grabbing one of the brochures for the School of International Relations, featuring the promotion for the second cohort of the International Scholar program starting in spring. Then, he pointed to an unopened tab on Nathaniel's screen.

"Oh, I'll be taking care of him shortly," Nathaniel tried to say convincingly. "First, I want to send out a follow-up email to our incoming replacements."

"Let's take care of him now, Nathaniel." Erik watched as Nathaniel scratched his head and took a sip of his drink at the tabletop. "Have you uploaded the new tests?"

"Yes, although they're less personal than the previous tests created by Nova. The information we already gathered provides plenty of insight to work with—"

"Nathaniel." Erik interrupted him sharply and stared with unblinking eyes until Nathaniel released a sigh and opened the tab. He typed in the password he created and gained access to Sebastian's brain microchip account that he had paused five months earlier. A three-dimensional hologram of a brain appeared beside categories that stored the data on Sebastian, such as for feelings detected, factors contributing to higher heart rates, sensory transference, pain indicators, and other checkpoints.

"He sure toughed it out, huh?" Erik remarked. "Did Nova test the others as harshly?"

Nathaniel darted his eyes upward to Jaewon's containers on the wall. "Yes," he said, offering nothing further. "We've never reactivated a dormant microchip in a subject, only in our models. As you can see here, Sebastian overcame most of the obstacles Nova tackled him with as she analyzed various functions, but we cannot understand why he did. We can only know the reasons behind a subject's success by understanding said individuals."

Erik let out a deep, boisterous laugh that echoed throughout the empty lab. "Our forces don't need to know why someone can or cannot withstand these tests. We need to know if it's possible and with what level of difficulty. That way, we know how to strengthen everyone in our forces. And the brain microchips won't do us any good in the heads of our enemies if they aren't capable of controlling or debilitating them. However, I think anyone who performs outstandingly well may see a different fate."

Nathaniel looked at the disabled status on Sebastian's brain microchip. He took his hands off the laptop touchpad, left the cursor hanging on the screen, and lifted his finger to the interactive hologram. He felt the weight of Erik's eyes as he clicked on "Reactivate," and the top of the brain emitted a glowing violet light.

In Brazil, Sebastian played a soccer game on a field with his old high school teammates in an aquamarine T-shirt, the center of which read "CBF." They were practicing together because a few, including Sebastian, were training to play the sport professionally. He ran down the field dodging opponents left and right, maneuvering the ball with such skill that his teammates made appraisal sounds. Approaching the opposing team's goal, he kicked the ball back and forth between his knees and headbutted it to a teammate.

As the ball hit his head, Sebastian felt an odd sensation course through his brain. He held onto his temples and rubbed circles counterclockwise to ease the tension. A high-pitched frequency startled him as a connection was made, symbolized by a short whiz. Sebastian wiped the sweat off his forehead and set determined eyes on the opposing team's goal, watching as his team's ball flew inside the net, followed by the rowdiness of his teammates celebrating their win.

It can't be. Nathaniel turned it off for me. He changed the password, and he wouldn't tell anyone. No, Sebastian tried to convince himself.

Nathaniel?

ACKNOWLEDGMENTS

A lifetime of passion for poetry and songwriting encouraged me to take the journey of writing my first book, and you all helped make it possible to share this story. Thank you so much for your support!

Brittney Revan	Sandra Pulido
Angélica Vega Aponte	Dominick Garatino
Jane Bailey	Eric Koester
Hafiza Kazi	Maria Brodeur
Noelle Eller	Sage Coates-Farley
Victoria Pulido	Taylor Robinson
Jennifer Russ	Patty Willets
Emily Ndiokho	Kelvin Riddick
Erin Beverley	Richard Ferreira
Jackson Beauregard	Rachel Lim
Kelly Marin	Brian Reed
Ashley Mahrer	Patrick Remick
Cindy Zheng	Tom Lieber
Anna Janson	Aditi Pillai
Graham Sak	Bryce Phillips
Alycia Kunkle	Christine Gettings
Nicholas Dawson	Ilia Epifanov
Madelyn Hoffman	Nick Guthman

Brooklynne Mosley

Mark Schneider

Wendy Stanton

Georgie Kiely

Geralyn Whitney

Thomas Esemplare

James Farrand

McPlante

Patricia Lanciano

Thomas Tsangarides

Gitika Harith

Sara Ameen

Jackson Yoder

Catherine Gordon

Miranda Niesman

Isi Holliday

Jasmine Brooks

Marianne Norman

Shawna Bruell

Matthew Skolar

Guadalupe Mabry

Robert Sicina

Olivia Freides

Veronica Pacheco

Cassia Efthymiou

Robert Satterthwaite

Alicia Brenner

Dino Iannelli

Savannah Hall